This is dedicated to all the caregivers, who give effortlessly, often placing their lives on hold and at risk, to care for those who can no longer care for themselves.

Let's not forget the Home Healthcare Nurses, family and friends who support the caregivers and lastly, the special people requiring care.

The Care Giver's Son

Outside the Window Looking In

Pp
PROSEPRESS
www.prosepress.biz

The Care Giver's Son
Outside the Window Looking In
Copyright © 2013
T. Allen Winn

All rights reserved. This publication may not be reproduced, stored in a retrieval system, or transmitted in any form: recording, mechanical, electronic, or photocopy, without written permission of the publisher. The only exception is brief quotations used in book reviews.

Published by Prose Press
Pawley's Island,
South Carolina 29585

proseNcons@live.com
www.prosepress.biz

ISBN: 978-0-9886194-6-3

Comments:
Cover design: OBD

Fiction by T. Allen Winn

<u>Trudy Wagner Detective Thrillers</u>
Road Rage
North of the Border
<u>The Bully Series</u>
Dark Thirty

In Memory

John Robert Bowie

Ruby Holmes Bowie

Mary Elizabeth Bowie Winn

Thomas Jefferson Winn

Special Thanks

Carol Jackson

Henrietta Timms

Edna Jones

Friends, Family, Supporters and Substitute Caregivers

Reverend Ray Massey

Reverend Ken Timmerman

Chandler-Jackson Funeral Home

Winning Photography

Chapters

11 My Papa

16 Have You Ever Been Fishing on A Hot Summer Day?

27 Falling from Grace

41 The Escape Artist

52 Tribute, My Way

64 Being Sociable While Kicking and Screaming

70 Life is What You Make It

93 Déjà Vu

107 Queen Solomon's Dilemma

124 The Double Sided Sword

129 The Caregiver's Caregiver

136 God's Plan

142 Raising the Window and Peeping Inside

149 Inside the Window Looking Out

- 162 Closing the Window but Opening My Eyes
- 167 Eating Crow is truly an Acquired Taste
- 171 Putting it into Words, Therapy for the Soul
- 174 Skinning the Rabbit (Bonus Short Story)

*Heroes are the people
Who do what has to be done
When it needs to be done,
Regardless of the consequences.*

The Care Giver's Son

Sitting on the balcony, overlooking the ocean, I should be content. I certainly feel content. It's Friday and three days short of Memorial Day, a long weekend away from work. I find myself in the driver's seat. Work can be dispelled until Tuesday. I really don't hate my job, so dread is not part of the equation.

I glance at my watch and it returns my stare, indicating the afternoon is still early at 7:45. Our oceanfront condo comes fully equipped with an ocean and a beach. The tenth floor offers the perfect view of both. I sip on my adult beverage of choice, Vodka and cranberry juice, while the May breezes feeding off the ocean create their own calming effect.

From my vantage point and comfortably positioned in my chase lounge, I gaze on the endless Atlantic Ocean. It reminds me of the deck side view from the countless cruises I have sailed. The waves lap endlessly at the shoreline. The width of the beach at Garden City has been reduced to less than twenty yards by the incoming tide.

Various oceanic birds soar in the skies below me. How odd it is to look down at birds in flight. People walk their various canines, oblivious to me in the catbird's seat. Dogs are such chick magnets. I should know. I once owned one of those poodle mixes, and yes they attracted females like flies on; well you know what draws flies.

Kicking back, I watch a family attempting to launch a kite. The kite isn't cooperating, flipping wildly loop to loop, refusing to go airborne. I observe that flying a beach kite requires the team effort of at least five or six people. Finally the eagle has been launched, and the crowd below cheers triumphantly. It's just a kite. Get over it. The simple things are often taken for granted; guilty as charged.

A lone surfer straddles her board, bobbing on the swells waiting for that perfect hang ten wave. I am caught in her web of solitude. We are one. She just doesn't know I'm part of hers. The young surfer girl finally calls it quits with the daylight dwindling. There will be no perfect wave this time. Perfection is never guaranteed, nor is life. Life doesn't come with a warranty. If you don't like it, you can't return it for a better one. You're stuck with what destiny holds for you. It seems so unfair.

It's funny, not ha-ha, that my thoughts would drift to her, after so long without thinking about her. I never sensed it approaching. It just happened. I remember how she had so enjoyed sitting on the balcony of our other beach condo in Windy Hill, not a care in the world, all her responsibilities left so far behind. She too had sipped on her own adult

The Care Giver's Son

beverage, forgetting about being there, and only about being here.

It comes in waves just like those crashing below, angry, relentless, and chipping away at my soul, like the grains of sand reclaimed by the ocean. Me, without my beach shovel and little sand bucket, I certainly didn't want to dig up the past. There is no buried treasure in my mind, and I really didn't wish to dig up old bones. Our mind doesn't always allow us perfect control, nor does our heart. They are double teaming me right now and winning handily.

Don't get me wrong. Remembering is not necessarily a bad thing; however, I would rather pick my own battles with the past, and not have them picked for me. Subconsciously, I guess I had made that choice. Now I must deal with the consequences.

I mentioned how sitting on the tenth floor, and gazing over the Atlantic, so reminded me of the view from a cruise ship. It, too, reminded me of her. She so loved cruising. She would rather be cruising than be on any other type of vacation. She had lured me onto my first cruise. It forever changed my life, all for the best of reasons.

How ironic, I just so happened to notice the mug on the table, holding my beverage of choice, display a Bermuda logo. I remember purchasing it on my only cruise to Bermuda, her second time, and a cruise she thoroughly enjoyed. Things happen for a reason, and apparently this one intended on triggering deeper memories of her for me. It certainly succeeded in doing so, hands down.

I have no regrets thinking about her. Sure, I haven't thought of her in quite a long time, at least not like this, but it's not because I wish to forget about the past. I just don't let it consume me like I once did. In some ways it doesn't seem like it has been five years since she left me, and in other ways it seems like forever.

A family below just caught my eye. A grandpa, entertaining his granddaughter, pretends to run from the approaching wave like one of those little sandpiper birds that follows the ebbing tide, afraid to get its feet wet. Other family members embrace, while posing for photographs. New memories were being made ten stories down, while I stumble through old memories from the seclusion high above.

I so miss her. She was supposed to be here with me, making memories of our own. A wave of anger passes over me. I find it so easy to question why she had to leave me, when I could not prevent the inevitable. Being here without her just isn't right. Why did I deserve to be cursed with a life without her? My anger subsides just as quickly. I can't really blame anyone for her being gone. I'd like to, but I can't. Wallowing in self pity isn't very pretty, even from this height.

In three days I will be fifty six. I am not a war veteran, but I will share the lime light this Memorial Day Monday with those who have given and suffered much more than I and I salute them. Where have all the years gone? Fifty six, she should still be here to help me celebrate and shoot off fireworks! What a silly thought. If she were here, shooting fireworks would not be on our agenda.

Stubborn, pigheaded and extremely opinionated, traits we tended to share. We certainly could engage in verbal, knock down, drag out battles. No, it never came to physical blows. Sometimes I think she enjoyed those confrontations, although she never admitted it. I didn't care to argue, but stubborn, pigheaded and opinionated, I couldn't avoid them either. We both thought we were always right. We were.

While I see her face and antics vividly, hearing her voice doesn't come so easily. I wish it did. Sometimes I dream of her, not as often as I once did. I wake up wishing the dreams had never ended. I have often wondered if dreams were portals to another time, another dimension; God's way of allowing us to connect with those not available by phone or e-mail.

She loved me before I recognized the meaning of the word. The first time she held me in her arms, she fell in love with me for who I was and would someday be. Much time would pass before I could return what she had given so freely and openly. Even after I finally made the connection, saying I love you wouldn't flow easily from my lips. Love isn't just words. Saying it isn't always necessary. Feeling it is everything.

The setting sun casts long condo shadows on the beach, as does an ever growing darkness and emptiness in my soul. I sip another drink from the Bermuda mug. The corners of my mouth turn upward with warming memories, triggering better times we spent together. I must look silly to the passing birds, smiling all alone on this balcony. Kodak moments are never squandered, now are they?

Taking a deep breath, I wipe a joyful tear from the corner of my eye, just as another one trickles down the opposite cheek. I catch it with the back of my right hand.

Some think that tears are unmanly but not me. I have shed my fair share. Hey, I'm on the tenth floor, so who is going to see them any way, not that I really care. I've never seen a bird be a snitch, unless maybe it's a Stool Pigeon.

The May darkness has finally lowered its curtain, and the cooler beach breeze chills my

The Care Giver's Son

bones. I decide it's time to head inside. I urgently have the desire to preserve my thoughts and feelings on the old lap top. I begin typing what I have experienced alone on that balcony, thinking happy birthday to me.

I just remembered how she had once been sitting here at the beach. Looking around I connect with two fish lamps in the small den, remembering that she had bought them for beach side decor. Sighing, I whisper I love you and miss you so. I receive no answer, but I know she has heard me. I hope she did.

My fingers freeze on the computer's keyboard. I hear the jiggling of a key and the condo door opening. The clock on my computer screen signals it is after nine. I turn to see my wife walking down the long tiled hallway. She has just arrived from her early afternoon girls' night out, to join me for the holiday weekend.

She smiles and we kiss. She doesn't ask me what I'm typing on the computer. She's accustomed to me spinning a fiction novel, knowing how I love to write. I haven't shared my writings with her or anyone else yet, nor have I taken that leap into the publishing world. This simply serves as my personal therapy for now. It's my time to heal.

She exits to the bathroom to freshen up. My thoughts return to my Mama, taken so suddenly by pancreatic cancer, dying three quick months after being diagnosed. Being an only child, it is tough not having her here to keep me on the straight and narrow, not that she really ever had a prayer, not with the way I have lived my life, stubborn, pigheaded and opinionated.

She was as much a friend to me as she was a Mom. We could talk about anything and often did. Looking much younger than her age and me looking older for mine, people who didn't know us sometimes mistook us for brother and sister. She loved those comments more than I did.

She died in my arms, sitting on the edge of her single bed as my dad, bedridden and silent, watched from his hospital bed. Their queen size bed long gone, their bedroom had been converted to accommodate their medical needs, one single bed for her, and one hospital bed for him. They shared the same bedroom to the bitter end.

Dad could no longer talk or do for himself, compliments of being ravaged by Alzheimer's and Parkinson. He was very alert and watching as his wife, his caregiver, left before him. I can't remember him being more alert and attentive, than he was when she struggled for her life, just across the room. His eyes were saying goodbye, even though the words couldn't form on his lips.

As only she could do, she looked into my eyes and said, 'I love you sweetie.' One quick

The Care Giver's Son

gasp for air and she was gone. I'm sure my dad understood what had just happened, but he just couldn't communicate his thoughts to us. He died three months later. Aspiration took him as we fed him his dinner in that very same room. Three months, they were gone. It doesn't seem fair. Unfortunately, I don't get to call the shots.

I believe Daddy was ready to join her. He had always been a fighter when she had been his caregiver. With her gone, he had no reason to be here with us. I honestly believe he longed to be with her. He is now, and his suffering is no more. With them both gone, I feel the wrath of suffering.

An only child bangs away on his keyboard, still hurting, as only an only can. My bloodline forever gone, but my memories are still in tact. The hurting never goes completely away as I have proven sitting out there on that balcony.

Writing and remembering is my passion and my escape from the very edges of the dark abyss called depression. I'm winning that battle for now but the war isn't over I fear. It is forever an uphill climb. I'm getting just a tad too old to take on such a steep slope. I'm more comfortable descending.

My beloved wife returns. We prepare to officially kick off our Memorial Day Weekend and make memories of our own. I close my laptop, sanity still in check, another one of life's chapters and lessons completed. I glance to the heavens and under my breath whisper I love you too, sweetie. The hurting festers always. I'm sure my wounds will eventually heal. I have to believe. Mama and Daddy would have expected me to move on without them.

We had always thought Mama would relocate with us to the beach someday. Who would have thought Dad with his many medical issues would have survived her. We made that journey without her. She completed a journey of her own. And now begins my journey, getting here from there wasn't so easy. My ending had a beginning and it starts now.

The Care Giver's Son

My Papa

It was late for the phone to be ringing; just after midnight. Phone calls at this hour generally don't equate to good news, or are usually wrong numbers. Being optimistic isn't one of my better attributes. I picked it up after the third ring, my wife, having already retired for the night, and apparently was not going to answer it. I'm not a phone person. That's why we have answering machines. Screening a call is more my forte. If it is important or urgent, you simply pick it up in the middle of the caller leaving their message, and if it isn't or is someone you don't want to talk to, you allow them to leave a message. What was I thinking by abandoning my normal strategy?

I mustered up a cordial greeting. "Hello," I recognized the caller's identity, which reinforced my suspicions. "Hey, Mama, is there anything wrong?"

"It's Daddy, he's taken a turn for the worst. You better come. I've called the doctor."

The tearful tone in her shaken voice told me that indeed it was the worst case scenario. Papa had been steadily going downhill for over a year now. Ninety years old, he had lived a long and fruitful life, but losing him was going to be the toughest thing I had ever endured up until now. Witnessing his health deteriorate had been extremely difficult for an only grandson to bear. I didn't particularly handle this sort of situation so well; not that anyone does.

I ended the call telling Mama I would be there as quickly as possible, and then I just leaned back on the couch and stared into space. I really didn't want to do this. I had forever dreaded this day. I could probably be at my grandparent's house in less than fifteen minutes. Even with Papa's declining health, Mama had insisted keeping him at home, with Granny, in familiar surroundings, with family close by his side. A nursing home was completely out of the question, end of discussion, no debate. She and Daddy were taking care of him, along with Granny. Daddy was retired and Mama's job was close by, so they made it work, along with help from family and friends.

There was but one thing missing in this setup, most of the time, me. I did my part, but typically I had to be asked. I do love my Papa, so doing what I must isn't the issue. Listen to me, 'doing what I must.' There lies the problem. Even I should have been smart enough to realize it, this should not have been a burden, but instead, a privilege. Procrastination set in. I didn't want to be there when he died, plain and simple. My wife came into the room,

The Care Giver's Son

wiping sleep from her eyes, asking me who had just called.

"It was Mama. She thinks Papa's time has come and wants us to come over."

"So why are you just sitting there?"

I didn't answer at first, so she asked me a second time. "I don't know. I just need time to think."

That was a stupid response and reaction to an urgent request by Mama. Papa is dying. Why was I not already in the car and heading there?

"I need a few minutes," I told her.

Minutes were precious and I was squandering them. My wife didn't push the issue, but she should have. Our relationship was strained, our marriage on the ropes, and she didn't come around family much anymore. I knew, eventually, I would be making the drive alone, even under these terrible circumstances. That didn't help my cause, but I wasn't about to ask her to go with me. Why would I? I didn't want to go either.

I grew up in Papa's shadow. He was the only granddad I had ever known in my thirty seven years muddling my way though life. I had one failed marriage and another on the brink, but neither situation really had anything to do with what I faced right now. Papa was on his death bed, and my family needed me. What none of them could possibly understand was that I wasn't ready to bury Papa, even though I realized this day had been fast approaching. Some would demonize me as being insensitive and uncaring. That's certainly their prerogative. I would be fueling that fire if I didn't get my butt in gear. My butt and I weren't ready.

Time slowed to a snail's pace, more my choice than that of the ticking clock. To be honest, I didn't want to see him take his last breath. That made it too final and real to me. Aren't we supposed to remember the good times? Seeing him die before my eyes would not leave a lasting good image in my mind. I'd rather remember him in truly wonderful times. He already no longer looked like that barrel chest man that had taken me under his wing, while my folks worked the second shift at the local textile mill. Why would I want to watch him die? People should have choices in these matters. We should respect a person's decision.

Southerners yearn to be around family when tragic circumstances warrant it. Our family was small. It wasn't like I could tag out and my replacement would jump into the ring. Nope, to the contrary, I was an only child, an only grandchild. I had successfully broken the chain thus far. I had no children, and not because I didn't want any. For whatever reason, life had not blessed me with one. My wife, as predicted, had returned to the bedroom, opting not to accompany me. While she had attempted to console me, even she knew that I couldn't be helped, prompted or persuaded to get my butt

The Care Giver's Son

in gear and take that ride. Plain and simple, this was tough.

I no longer sat on the couch. Pacing had overcome me. I was quite an excellent pacer too. Walking about prevented me from doing the needful, and driving to where they expected me to be. I stepped outside; figuring fresh air might clear my head. Foot propped up and gazing at a sky speckled with stars, I had the crap scared out of me. Sheba, our indoor-outdoor cat rubbed against the back of my leg. Colorful language spewed from my lips, echoing across the hollow. I reached down and petted the feline, having felt like I were the one who had forfeited one of my nine live; that is, if I was a cat.

I sat down in an old aluminum chair, its fabric strapping worn and faded. It was our version of southern porch furniture. Sheba leapt into my lap. This time I saw her coming. I scratched her behind her ears, and ran my hand along her sleek body. She purred her gratification. I thought about Papa, not the one possibly breathing his last breath, but instead one of my fondest memories, the bull of a man, still healthy and casting the shadow for me to stand within. I hated this situation. I didn't want to go over there right this very minute. I couldn't avoid the inevitable forever, could I? I tried replacing dread with happy thoughts.

T. Allen Winn

Have you ever been fishing on a hot summer day?

"Honey, this is the way you bait your hook," Papa said, jabbing the curved spur hook through the red wiggler, looping it, spearing it a second, and then a third. The worm squirmed, but stayed knotted to the hook, Papa showed me how to cast the line, affixed to my cane pole, tossing the fish food into the water.

I was six years old and this was my first time to go fishing and actually fish, instead of watch. The cane pole was too long and too heavy for me to hold it upright. Papa had found a forked limb, shredded off the leaves, and had then cut it to the correct length with his pocket knife. He then stuck the sharpened opposite end into the ground. It protruded from the ground, the v-shape served as the perfect stand to elevate and rest my cane pole. He then gave me one simple instruction. 'Watch the red and white cork bobbing in the water. If it goes under the water, Hon, you have a fish on your line.'

I looked over at Papa. He had baited his own cane pole and tossed his line in the water. I watched the bald headed man in denim overalls, mimicking his actions. Slick headed and only a few sparse teeth in his mouth, he was in his element. Fishing was not a sport, but

The Care Giver's Son

rather a way of life, something that put food on the table. Most anything caught on a hook was a keeper, and would batter up nicely in a frying pan. Today's catch of choice would be Catfish. I wasn't sure how catfish knew they were supposed to take the bait. The early fish gets the worm, I suppose. I continued to watch my cork, mostly motionless for now.

Papa didn't just sit on the bank quietly. He often sang to the fish. I think most of his tunes were made up, but it didn't really matter. He would belt one out and we'd both laugh. Unlike hunting, fishing didn't require us to sit motionless and quiet. I was certainly glad. I could squirm worse than one of those worms on a hook. He sang one of my favorites.

Have you ever been fishing,
on a hot summer day?
Watch the little bitty fishes
As they jump and play.
With your hands in your pockets
And your pockets in your pants,
Watch the little bitty fishes
Do the shimmy-shimmy dance.

Now that was just too funny. Papa nodded towards the water.

"You got a bite," he said.

Sure enough, my cork was moving. It would bob a couple of times then stop, and then bob slightly again. Papa told me to wait until the cork went under the water, and then yank the line. The cane pole was still propped on its wood stand. How was I going to yank something I couldn't even hold up by myself? I had no time to think. The cork disappeared, the end of the pole now bending.

"You got him," yelled Papa "Now bring him in, Hon."

He hadn't exactly taught me that technique yet. So I had hooked my first fish, so what now? I grabbed the pole with both hands and attempted to pick it up. I only succeeded in dislodging it from its wood holder. It flopped onto the ground, most of it splashing into the water. I did the only thing I knew to do. I began backing up, dragging the pole. Papa just laughed, clapped his hand on his knee and let me go at it. If I was going to catch my first fish, I was going to do it with no help from him, so it seemed.

I continued inching backwards, dragging the pole, with two thirds of it now out of the water. The cork was nowhere to be seen, and something on the end of that line wasn't happy about me pulling it towards the bank. This was tug of war, boy against fish. It called for a new strategy. I turned, with my back now to the pond. I tucked the cane pole under my arms and then gripped it, and began walking as fast

The Care Giver's Son

as I could in the opposite direction. I was making better headway. Papa just laughed and watched me do battle with my watery foe.

I stumbled forward, losing my balance. I had to let the pole drop if I didn't want to end up with a mouth full of grass. I stopped my fall with my knees and palms.

"You got him," yelled Papa "And he's a nice'un."

Getting to my feet, I turned to see the monster flopping on the bank. He had a huge head, long whiskers and big ole mouth opening and shutting. My fish line had vanished inside its mouth. I eased up to take a closer look. It was slick, with bluish skin. Papa said it was a Blue Cat, probably at least five or six pounds. It was indeed big, at least by my six year old standards. I could see the pride beaming in Papa's sparkling eyes and almost toothless smile. I had caught my first fish, a nice'un, and I had done it by myself. It had been by design, his, that I land it with no help.

Sheba nudging my hand, craving more rubbing, jarred me from la-la land. I sucked in a deep breath, dread creeping over me again. I should be going, I knew that, but still I struggled to make that very first step. I didn't want to see Papa dying. I wanted to remember him living. I had good memories. Why would I want to muddy up the water with bad ones? Late night phone calls come to no good. I'd better go before getting that second one.

T. Allen Winn

Without telling my wife, I made my way to the yard, and mustered up the willpower to sit behind the wheel of my car. It's so very simple. Just insert the key into the ignition and turn the switch. It's not like I hadn't done it a million times. I started the car and was on my way.

The roadway was dark and deserted. It matched my somber mood perfectly. My headlights caught sight of a rabbit darting across the road, frantically trying to avoid the wheels of my car. I helped by veering. The rabbit avoided being road kill this time. I remembered going rabbit hunting with Papa. I was too young to carry a gun but I walked beside him, stride for stride; maybe two to his every one now that I think about it. I can hear those beagles running, a rabbit having been jumped. We kept pace, moving toward the sounds of the yelping dogs. Eventually they'd turn the rabbit and aim it back in our direction. I never did quite understand how they knew how to do that.

The barking became louder, the dogs closer. Papa motioned me to stand behind him at the edge of a clear cut bordering a briar thicket. The thunder from his shotgun made me flinch. I was always too late in covering my ears. One shot, one rabbit, Papa never missed, or at least I never saw him miss. I never did understand why having a rabbit's foot was supposed to bring the owner good luck. The rabbit Papa held up by its hind legs had four of them. It

The Care Giver's Son

didn't look so lucky to me. Papa gathered up the dogs to his side and we began walking to the next thicket. Soon, we jumped another rabbit and the beagles were in hot pursuit.

I approached the traffic light. This was my turn to Papa and Granny's house. Dread crept over me. This was not where I wanted to be or what I wanted to be doing. Mama didn't seem to mind. She did this every day, taking care of him. Saying she didn't mind probably wasn't the right thing to think. This was her daddy after all. It had to be tough on her seeing him this way also, but I still didn't want to see him die. I didn't want that image in my head. I loved him and had loved everything about him. My heart skipped a beat. I recognized the doctor's car parked out front. Several other cars were there too. Just how many people had Mama phoned? Maybe she had called them after I hadn't showed up.

I pulled on the curb and parked behind the others. I turned off the ignition and gripped the wheel. I was on the verge of hyperventilating. I didn't want to do this. Every light in the four room mill hill house was on, and I could see shadows moving about through the closed shades. The car door felt like I was pushing open a massive steel gate. I swung one leg out and then the other. They both felt like lead. It took all I could muster to will them to move. One step, then another, just keep going, I told myself. The steps leading up to the front porch appeared endless and so steep.

My life somehow felt like the steepest of climbs. This certainly was no place for a pity party, but delaying what I dreaded facing, I could so easily be distracted. I stopped and looked at the white vinyl mill house. By design it matched many others on the surrounding streets. Textile mills were noted for their mill villages back in the day, that time long before I was born. These houses had been built by the mill's owners, and then rented to the workers. They were built all around the mill, intentionally within walking distance. If you lived in one, you were expected to work in the mill. Whole families abided by that unwritten commitment. My grandparents and parents worked for the local mill. I broke that cycle, and only because my parents insisted that I would never work in one.

It was hard work, often long hours and not the greatest pay, but it was a way to make a descent living, most would say. Eventually, those living in the houses had an opportunity to buy them. Many did. My grandparents had bought this one. This house was the only place I had ever known them to live. The old house now had central air and heat. I can still smell that old cast iron coal burning stove, heating half the house. An oil heater, when used, heated the other half. In summers, a specialty built window fan was mounted in the only kitchen

The Care Giver's Son

window. The fan forced the inside air out and sucked the fresh outside air in, through any open windows. Papa and granny never complained about the heat or the cold. It was just weather.

Papa was inside, and in a bad way. Yet, I still stood my ground outside, reminiscing the good times, dreading the bad, those that waited for me at the top of the steps. It was quiet and peaceful here. That's the way it always felt here. It was a home, not a house. Love and tender care ensured it always remained that way. Inside, oh yes, inside, all was not well. My feet may as well be locked in a slab of cement for all it was worth. I remained frozen in place, a virtual time warp within my own brain. I didn't want my Papa to die but the man inside had not been my Papa for a long time now.

Mama had chosen to care for him, to keep him here; not because she had to, but because she wanted to do it. I'm not so sure I could have made that call if that decision would have rested on my shoulders. Possibly the concept of unconditional love eluded me. I was a mutant, a skip in the gene pool, more suited for thinking about what best worked for me and not those of others. I'm standing here still. I rest my case. I willed my right foot onto the first step, and then my left. Surely incremental maneuvers are better than none at all. How much time had expired since Mama had phoned me? I refused to glance at my watch and verify my suspicions.

Funny how most of my memories of time spent with Papa involve fishing and hunting. He was more than that to me, but I can't help it. I just had a fleeting thought of squirrel hunting. Papa probably took me squirrel hunting more times than I dare attempt to count. I smiled, thinking about those times we would sit on the side of a hill in a hardwood hollow, waiting for the furry tailed critters to show up. Papa would position us near an old oak dropping acorns or a bountiful hickory nut tree. We sat and waited for that first sound of rustling leaves.

The gun would echo and the squirrel would be no more. "Sit still, Hon, let them come to us." He would remember where the critter lay and would wait on the next one. Squirrels either have short memories or are just really stupid, because another, then another would show up, nearly in the same spot. Papa never missed. Granny would be cooking dumplings or fried squirrel this afternoon, Papa would say. I must admit, it was good eating. Of course, I grew used to eating wild critters. They all tasted good to me. No, they didn't taste like chicken.

Papa never was a deer hunter. I'm not sure why he wasn't but he hunted most everything else. Doves and quail were on the menu when in season. To me, both were too quick and not much meat on their bones. I never tried quail hunting, but once, and only once, I did go dove

The Care Giver's Son

hunting down in the low country, at Adams Run. As memory serves me, I shot over two dozen times at those soaring little speed demons and only bagged one. I really only winged it. A cousin had to finish it off for me.

Not everything Papa pursued required a gun or fishing pole. He was quite the grappler. I'll have to take his say so on this because he never took me grappling, but I have seen the results of his technique. Grappling, for those who are not familiar with the term, is when you wade in a river and reach blindly underneath rocks, logs or the river bank and catch critters with your hands. Papa mostly went grappling for snapping turtles. Why someone would want to risk having their fingers snapped by a turtle defies logic, but that was Papa. He caught some big'uns, so he would say.

The creaking of the front door shocked me back to the present. Daddy stood there, staring at me and motioning for me. He had no way of knowing I had been here for a while. It would be my little dirty secret.

"What took you so long?"

I just sort of shrugged. I had no valid explanation, so why lie about it. He hugged me when I reached him. Daddy wasn't a hugger. His side of our family wasn't huggers.

Mama's side of the family hugged everyone, whether they knew you or not. His hug made me think only bad thoughts. Dad, one of few words too, merely said, "He's gone."

T. Allen Winn

Gone, what was that supposed to mean? Papa had skipped out. He had been doing that a lot before he had become totally bedridden. Maybe Mama had jumped the gun. As the dementia had taken a foothold, Papa had started sneaking from the house. Under normal conditions he could barely walk, having two bad knees. Standing on that front porch, I wavered, my mind shifted to better times, my escape route. Daddy stepped back inside. I was supposed to follow him.

The Care Giver's Son

Falling from Grace

The front porch, many a Sunday afternoon we had spent sitting on that porch. Growing up, it had been a tradition to come to their house after church. Granny always cooked for an army, regardless of how many were expected for dinner. My favorites were her potato salad, a side dish and either the banana pudding or lemon pie for dessert. She took time and care preparing all three dishes, no short cuts, no imitations, the read deal every time. The potato salad wasn't sweet, the desserts were. I always made sure I took helpings of each home with me, and I must confess these were mine and nobody else's. I didn't share them very often.

I could envision Papa rocking in one of those chairs or swinging in the porch swing. We watched the traffic pass by, waving at everyone of course. It is a genuine southern tradition to wave at vehicles, whether you know the folks inside or not. Same goes for people walking along the road or on the sidewalk. Northerners don't grasp that concept. The other highlight of the day would be viewing the couple of trains that passed by over the trestle, two blocks away. It was always worth the ogling to see what sorts of things were being transported on the various rail cars. Papa would often identify them out loud; new automobiles, army vehicles, rail car loads of coal, and so on. That overpass had minimal clearance. I can't count the times vehicles, too high or overloaded, crashed into that trestle, overturning or becoming lodged underneath.

I had managed to climb the dozen or so steps, and stood on the gray painted porch. I braced myself with my hand on the wrought iron railing. I absolutely didn't want to do this, but Daddy had seen me. I dreaded either outcome; finding him already dead or being there when he drew his last breath. I hated funerals far worse. The few I have attended, and believe me when I say it, there have only been a handful; I just didn't get it. I don't go to them unless I have no other choice. It just doesn't seem natural to me to wait your turn in line so you can peek inside the coffin and view the dead.

Dead is dead. We know the person is deceased so why do I need to look inside their last resting place to confirm it. Oh how I hate those dreaded comments. *She or he looked so good, natural and at peace.* Is being dead looking natural and at peace, only if they had been suffering, maybe. Or we get the flip side; *he or she didn't look like themselves*. Dead isn't sleeping, so how do you think you're supposed to look? No one practices for this final stage of their life. There's no dress rehearsal.

What really *gets my goat*, are people standing around making this out to be a social function. They're seeing people they haven't seen in forever, laughing and having a good ole time reminiscing, and not necessarily about the deceased, and forgetting why they are there in the first place, to pay their last respect. Mama is not one who goes to funeral either, so I inherited my belief honestly. Furthermore, she professes, *if you can't take the time to come visit me while I'm alive, I don't want you coming around and gawking over my open casket.* She has profoundly stated she does not want an open viewing when she has met her maker and wants a quick funeral; none of these days of mourning before they plant her in the ground. She can often be a wise lady.

Delay tactics, I'm avoiding the inevitable. I grabbed the door handle and need to do this. I was but a mere storm door and wood entrance door that kept me from determining Papa's status. I was running out of ways to milk my procrastination. I sucked in as much oxygen as I could one last time and blew it back out, and then made my grand entrance. Two of my cousins standing in the den told me what I needed to know. Papa was with the angels. In a way I was relieved, but I didn't dare say that out loud. My cousins hugged me and patted me on the back, telling me how sorry they were, with tears flowing freely. Oddly, I didn't cry, but I hadn't faced Mama yet.

Daddy had announced I had arrived and Mama made her way through the kitchen to the den. Mill houses are of simple design. Envision a square box and place four rooms inside it. I entered the den from the front porch. The kitchen was next. Take a right and you were in the bedroom and another right and you were in what they called, the front room or living room, with a couch hideaway bed. Both the den and living room were in the front and the bedroom and kitchen were in the back. Exit the kitchen to an enclosed back porch and bathroom. Streets around the textile mill were lined with houses of similar floor plans.

Mama had been crying and cut loose again when she saw me. "He's gone. What took you so long to get here?"

I should have calculated my response, had given it more thought, instead of blurting out, "I didn't want to be here when he died."

Mama released me just as quickly as she had embraced me. She gave me **THE LOOK**. "You needed to be here."

I had no defense except I didn't want to be here, but I didn't repeat my conviction. It was obvious she didn't share my feelings nor did she bother to understand them. In her eyes, it was absolutely my responsibility to have been here for her and the rest of the family. Next, Mama spoke that dreaded statement, "Would you like to see him before they move him? He's in the bedroom."

Why would I want to view my Papa, dead in his bed? It sounds just too morbid for my taste. This was coming from the same woman who doesn't want people viewing her cold dead

The Care Giver's Son

body in a coffin. I declined the invitation, waving her off, mumbling something incoherent. I'll hand it to her. The caregiver had stayed true to her commitment. She had made sure Papa passed on to the great beyond, in his house, in his bed, surrounded by family and friends, with the exception of me. That exception part still stuck in her craw, and she wasn't going to allow it to simply fade away. I was her only son and I was supposed to have been by her side, right there in that bedroom when Papa breathed his last breath.

Ironically, I had not shed a tear yet, and not because I wasn't hurting. Actually I was hurting on extreme levels. I could hardly breathe. Bottling up feelings such as these inside probably isn't healthy. My chest and throat felt as if they were about to explode. True to my demeanor, I remained basically expressionless. That didn't mean I was heartless and didn't care, but explain that to Mama. She wasn't getting it. I had come off as a great disappointment. Then again, she had always wanted me to be somebody I wasn't, and I had the emotional scars to prove it. All my life I had been compared to other people, often portrayed as an underachiever or as someone who simply didn't care about anything. I reckon I get that from Daddy's side of the family. They're not very emotional either. Mama's side of the family is a different story.

Granny emerged from the bedroom. She spotted me and quickly embraced me. She confirmed that Papa was gone. Unlike Mama, she did not chastise me for not making it in time. She was simply glad I was there. She did encourage me to go visit him, but I declined her offer too. I just wasn't ready for this. Why didn't they just leave me alone and let me deal with it my way, on my terms, when I was ready. One thing about me, the harder you push me, the more I resist. Like I've said, pig headiness is a trait I definitely inherited from Mama, and we were indeed *two pigs in a poke*.

I felt like my life force was being sucked out of me. I couldn't bear being in this house, with him dead in the other room. I have no phobias and I'm not afraid of the dead, but this was **MY PAPA**, my only one and now he was gone. A piece of me was gone too. Force feeding me to comply with the stereotype of a bereaving grandson was not going to work. My band marches to its own drummer. The mood here was suffocating me. I realized I wasn't cut out to be a caregiver. The stakes were too high and the responsibilities were too great. Mama was in her element, but I hadn't inherited her compassion for these situations.

Daddy more mirrored my mood, with one exception; he had been here to the very end. He had also openly shared caregiver duty with Mama, never questioning or regretting his involvement. He remained quiet and on the

The Care Giver's Son

sidelines. He patted me on the back and did choke back some tears. It was tough to watch him displaying real emotion, because I had rarely ever seen it from him. He held things inside too. So far this had been going as badly as I had expected. Tonight we mourn, I suppose, and then at some point, we'll remember the good times. For me, escape was remembering the good times right now, not later. While I didn't openly share these, I did escape to my world where Papa and I shared granddad-grandson adventures. I slipped off to myself and visited that time before now. I never lacked for a vivid imagination and the walk though life with Papa had been unforgettable.

The folks from the funeral home had arrived and hauled Papa away. It was daylight and the somber mood had somewhat diminished. Well, it had for most of the others. I still suffered in my little world, searching for a way out, a lifeline that would bring me closure. One good thing, if there is a good thing in times like these; Mama and Daddy could return to some semblance of normalcy. Getting here from there had been a challenge.

Papa had suffered from dementia and that alone had made our lives interesting. Growing old, we expect the body to go, but too often our want to and can do no longer cooperate. The mind says yes, the body says I don't think so. It's much tougher when the body can do and the mind can't remember how. None of us had experienced the challenges of dealing with someone who no longer remembered us. Papa and his dementia had exposed us to a world we never knew existed. It was tough to look into Papa's eyes and see a confused man staring back, one who didn't know who I was and no longer remembered that very first catfish I had landed.

Caregiver wasn't really a familiar term back then, either. Mama did what she felt was right. She had been taking care of Granny and Papa all her life. Granny's medical condition seemed to have always had its ups and downs, more downs from listening to Mama. The only child stepped up to the plate at an early age, foregoing much of her childhood, assuming the adult role. Compound that with how protective Granny could be and Mama didn't have the opportunities I had of actually being allowed to be a kid. Looking back, maybe that's why she allowed me to be a kid and didn't burden me with too many rigorous responsibilities. In hindsight did it really help or hurt me in the long run? The saga will most certainly play out. Challenges a plenty lurked in my future. Papa's fall from the pedestal I had placed him on didn't happen overnight. Like any progressive disease, changes were gradual, almost unnoticeable at first until you began connecting the dots. As we reach those golden years, and if we have our heath and remain on this side of the dirt, we're ahead of the game, right? Health is such a relevant term. What good is a bull of a body if the mind has transformed into Silly Putty. Cruel thoughts, I agree, but facts are facts. It's not a pretty sight to witness.

All was not gloom and doom. If you can't spin some humor into the one's life that is spiraling out of control, then you're just going to be sucked into the vortex. Once you've allowed yourself to be caught in that swirling mess, it's tough to escape it. I had always been good at dancing around the edges of the cliff. Sure, I'd take a quick peek over the edge, but no way was I going to fall into the pity hole. My issue, or the issues many would have with me, was that I didn't openly embrace the care provider role. I wanted Papa to be my Papa at all cost. I had walked in his shadow. He wasn't what some might call a hero, but he was bigger than life to me.

Looking back now, the signs were probably there. Papa's driving skills had diminished. Approaching the ripe old age of eighty, those skills are impacted and expected to be compromised, so that alone wasn't a reason to wave the red flag. So he had a few fender benders with trees or other stationary objects that weren't able to jump out of his way. A dent here and there, a scrunched up tail gate on his truck, nothing that couldn't happen to any of us, right? No other vehicles had been in his crosshairs, or at least none that we knew of. He did begin complaining that because of two bad knees he was experiencing problems with the clutch and brake operation on his old truck. Bad knees could have been Papa's excuse to mask his forgetfulness. One has to wonder now.

Hunting and fishing, his passions, fell by the wayside. I tried taking him hunting, but I couldn't bury my head in the sand; his feebleness was evident. Assisting him to and from the woods wasn't so easily accomplished. Sadly, his mind may have been handicapping the process more, but none of us were thinking that way. Problem solved, I began setting rabbit boxes for him, and eventually I began dressing and preparing the critters for the stew pot.

He'd tell me wild tales of his long departed cronies, keeping me in stitches about their many encounters with nature's wild kingdom. With age, it isn't unusual to remember those times of things of times long forgotten and forget you haven't taken a bath today. No alarm bells signaled, *Houston we may have a problem*. Me, I'd offer a friendly jab when the tales became too bizarre, and we'd laugh together; not sure which of us was happier to let it slide.

Granny picked up on more than we did. He had begun misplacing things; not just simple items, but items more pertinent to his everyday life. His wallet began disappearing and eventually materializing in the oddest places. Papa would claim some harebrain excuse and

The Care Giver's Son

laugh it off. He never went anywhere without his trusty pocket knife. It had vanished. Papa said someone had stolen it. Sadly, we had no suspects. It would show up eventually, we told him, but it never did.

Granny depended on Papa doing the lion share of the grocery shopping. Neither of them could read nor write very well, a generation thing for their era. Schooling wasn't high on the priority list in their day. Kids had chores to do to support the family, often their education taking a backseat. Not to worry, Granny would draw pictures on the grocery list to assist Papa with his shopping. These were simple, not artistic by any stretch of the imagination, but an effective tool just the same.

Oddly, Papa began returning from grocery runs with very few of the items Granny needed. Even stranger, he would be gone for twice as long as normal. Speculation now, Papa must have been experiencing bouts of dementia; either he had forgotten his mission or maybe even his way. Granny would scold him and send him back to the store, or Mama or Daddy would pick up the items for her. An entire family fell into the trap of masking the greater problem. It's the easier road traveled. Me, I flitted along on the fringes, mostly not impacted by these frequent occurrences. I was much better at taking care of me, than worrying about anyone else's needs. I was the most important thing in my universe. Ask me if you have any doubts.

The brick wall eventually leapt in front of them. Granny, Mama and Daddy ran head on, crashing into it. The wreck could no longer be avoided. Papa had become paranoid. People were invading his life, entering his house and stealing his stuff. It was funny at first, not so funny when he couldn't be convinced otherwise. We had someone to blame now. We didn't know who that somebody was, but we did know they were ruthless and expressed no mercy when it came to these strangers wanting his stuff. Oddly, no one bothered Granny's belongings. The thief had but one motive; take his. There was no convincing him otherwise.

Mama and Granny decided to take Papa's truck keys. They feared for him and those on the roadways. It was just too funny how they blamed the absence of his keys on those very same culprits stealing his stuff. Papa bought it, but was still none too happy about forfeiting his ride. Granny eventually gave me the keys and truck, out of sight and out of mind, he would soon forget about his sixty one Chevy pick-up. If he, by some chance, remembered and asked, we'd just blame those sneaky people. He never did. It was as if it never existed. My Papa was drifting further from shore, in a boat with no paddle, no life preserver and little hope of stepping on dry land again. The real world had passed him by, a man with no island.

The Care Giver's Son

Mama, the family caretaker, embraced her role, enlisting Daddy's help, who had recently retired from the textile mill. Daddy had earned the right to enjoy life after over forty years in the dreaded cotton mill, as it was called. He had begun playing golf a couple of days a week with his buddies and for once didn't have to deal with the everyday stress the grueling job had bestowed on him. He had never known but one speed, wide open. It was nice to see him gearing things down, or at least as geared down as he could muster.

Don't get me wrong; Daddy dearly loved and respected Papa, and would do anything for the man, but even he was now going above and beyond the call of duty. His life was being impacted by Papa's declining health. Mama leaned on him and Daddy never complained. Me, I allowed them to. Somehow I was able to justify them doing it and not me. Papa, because of his bad knees, depended on a cane to get about, so just how much trouble could he really be, I thought.

Soon, not only were those people stealing from Papa, they began showing up just before dark. Papa was in their house, and he was convinced that they would not appreciate him being there once they arrived back home. There was no convincing him otherwise. He expressed an urgency to vacate the premises before they returned or there would be hell to pay. Those bad knees that stymied his mobility,

T. Allen Winn

no longer hampered him. A man on a mission, he was suddenly quite spry and extremely agile. It was good to see him active and apparently in no physical discomfort, but it came with consequences.

While one Papa re-emerged, another version vanished before my very eyes. I wasn't sure which one was the lesser of the two evils. The resurrected Papa could be quite entertaining but too unruly. The old Papa could be contained, but required too much of the hands on to ensure his daily existence. The re-invented version could not be trusted, we soon discovered. Choose your poison, so they say. I took the low road. Call me if you need me, and I'll see if I can work you in. I wasn't caregiver material by a long shot. Mama held that position nicely, so why rain on her parade. Why mess with perfection? Following the leader was my game of choice.

The Escape Artist

Papa might go from Jekyll to Hyde in the blink of an eye. One minute he was there and the next he was gone. One particular time, Granny couldn't locate him anywhere in the four room house, so she panicked and phoned Daddy. He was after all retired and was the caregiver on call, so to speak, while Mama still worked in the very same textile mill. Daddy arrived within ten minutes and spotted Papa two houses away, up the back alley, talking with a neighbor. Actually, the conversation Papa was having with the neighbor made no sense. The neighbor, respecting the elder, never let on that anything was out of the ordinary. He simply played along with Papa, something others would find difficult to do.

Daddy escorted him back to the house. Granny scolded Papa upon his return. He proceeded in cursing her like a salty old sailor, language no one had ever heard him use. Who was this vulgar man in Papa's body? This would not be the first or last in such curse word laced outbursts. Papa was becoming less Papa with each passing day. I was withdrawing even more, determined to not bear witness to his demise. I didn't want my images of Papa to be tarnished by this man now possessing his body. It just wasn't right. Call me if you need me, though, and I'll be there, if I don't already have something more pressing on my agenda. My motto, Mama and Daddy could probably handle it. There were two of them, right, and I'm just not cut out for this hands on care. So wrong, I know.

Papa had escaped out the back door just one time too many. Those dilapidated old knees were somehow transformed into bionic transplants. He could be out that door and down those half dozen steps, making haste his escape before you realized Elvis had left the building. This called for preventative actions. The door locked conventionally guaranteed nothing. Daddy installed a latch type lock, one that could be bolted just inches from the top of the door. Granny was taller and could reach it. Papa, less mobile and shorter, couldn't.

Where there is a will, there is a way. When Papa's alter ego emerged, he didn't lack on resourcefulness, especially when he needed to exit the premises before those owners returned. He would undergo a MacGyver transformation and improvise. Papa had vanished once again. Granny was perplexed as to how he had escaped this time. The neighbor, now in the loop, brought him back. The battle didn't stop there. Daddy and Granny talked until they were blue in the face, discouraging him from leaving a second time.

Just how was he unlocking that door? This called for a covert operation. Daddy and Granny pretended to not take notice when he slipped from the den, to the kitchen and

The Care Giver's Son

standing at that locked back door. Daddy smiled and nudged Granny as they watched Papa use his trusty cane to reach the latch, and slide the bolt to the open position. Daddy intercepted him, but he unleashed his barrage of uncharacteristic, vulgar laced language on Daddy. While it hurt him to be cursed like that from the man he admired, he took it in stride, and escorted him back to the den. They confiscated his cane. This didn't deter him from returning to the locked door, but without it, he could not escape.

We all laughed about the amazing Houdini and his feat, now that it had been thwarted. Caregiver includes being a jail keep and possessing extremely thick skin. Unfortunately, in this case, the house became Papa's prison, a sad ending indeed. Daddy didn't cherish his new occupation, prison guard. Mama continued her vigil as primary caregiver; determined to keep Papa in his house and not in a nursing home. I volunteered for nothing, a role perfectly suited for me. Papa became less Papa with each passing day. I missed my Papa, the one I tried desperately to envision and remember, the hunter, the fisherman.

Good news, Papa could now be confined. Bad news, he became more belligerent and unmanageable, especially as the evening's darkness approached. Very persistent, he needed to leave before those other people arrived back home. He couldn't allow them to catch him in their home. He could not be convinced otherwise that he was in his house, not theirs. This called for new strategy. Mama, the head honcho caregiver, devised a new plan. She and Daddy loaded Papa up in their Lincoln Town Car and took him for a spin. By merely offering him an olive branch and escape plan, the gesture hushed him up and eased his concerns. Papa transformed into the perfect passenger on a ride to nowhere.

Mama's deceitful plan worked perfectly. After riding Papa around for nearly an hour, they returned to his house. He recognized it for what it was, his home and not one belonging to strangers. His phobia had a name, Sundowners Syndrome, another new term for our little band of newbie's. He would be driven to the brink almost every afternoon as the shadows invaded his world, the sun setting and prompting those people to return to their house. An afternoon ride became a common practice. At the mere mention, Papa was up and heading to the backdoor. Mama and Daddy would alternate being the designated driver, riding him here and yonder, killing enough time to pave the way back to that little mill house he had once called home.

Even caregivers require downtime. Mama and Daddy took a weekend trip with friends. I was placed on standby, the designated fill-in person. Shortly after arriving home on Friday afternoon from my first shift job, I prepared

The Care Giver's Son

myself for a normal weekend. Not accustomed to my new found position, it would soon evolve into anything but normal.

Fridays was my kick back day, all about me after the end of a work week. I hadn't given it that much thought to what I was expected to do. The phone call came shortly after I arrived home and altered my usual plans. This would not be my normal lead into a weekend.

Granny asked me why I hadn't stopped by her house after work. I guess I had missed that section on my marching orders. I was in standby mode, not stand in. Granny sounded frantic. Papa had already begun his pacing and fretting about those people coming home and catching him in their house. Darkness arrived early in the dead of winter, so did Sundowners. I wasn't necessarily a happy camper, but I had agreed to do this, so I hopped in the car and headed to their house, *a riding we would go*.

The short drive gave me an opportunity to reflect, and not about me for a change. I envisioned the Papa of the past, full figure, filling out those Camel Overalls. I could see and hear that toothless laugh. I could smell the Papa bodily odor, a working man's fragrance. I remembered when I was just a tiny pup, how I would stay overnight with my grandparents, all of us sleeping in one room, heated by a pot belly coal burning stove. I'd wake to the sound of Papa stoking the fire, stirring up those coal embers, adding some fresh kindling, and then a scoop or two of coal, to knock the chill from our bones. There was something wonderful about smelling that coal fire. The only other heat in the house was from the oil heater in the front room, the living room, spare sleeping quarters, with the hideaway bed in the couch.

Part of the daily ritual was taking the coal bucket outside to the mountain of black rock piled in a corner next to the house, and filling it to replenish the spent ones in the stove. I'd pace Papa, stride for stride, eager to do my part. He'd let me load the bucket, but it was too heavy for me to carry. My job was to bring in an arm load of wood kindling. Papa would chop the wood with his ax, converting the large wood into thin slivers of kindling. I was too young to handle sharp objects, so I was the designated kindling gatherer-totter. I tended to take my responsibilities more seriously back then.

Oh yeah, Papa would allow me to do a little fire stoking too. I guess that's why I can't keep my poker out of the fireplace to this very day. Actually, I inherited The Original Poker from Papa. It was a gem, a hand crafted one forged by Papa's hands; black iron, twisted several times to give it character and a looped end for hanging. It was a man's fire poker, not one of those wimpy ones that come in a three piece fireplace kit. Papa no longer needed it after they finally installed electric heat and cooling. The installation also made the window fan unit

The Care Giver's Son

obsolete. Remember, it was inserted in the kitchen window and pulled the warm air from the house during those hot summer months and sucked in the night's air from any open windows. This was the technology before attic fans.

I pulled up on the curb in front of their house. I could see Granny standing in the doorway. She opened the door before my feet had touched the payment. She had that worried expression. Granny was the most religious woman I have ever known, but she was a chronic worrier. I'm not sure why her faith didn't kick in and prevent her from stressing out over every little thing. It made it tough on Mama growing up to have a normal childhood with Granny fretting over every little thing. She treated me the same way when I was a kid.

A mountain trip to the Great Smokey Mountains with Granny and Papa, when I was probably nine or ten, had fretful consequences for Granny. I accompanied them and an Uncle and Aunt on their annual trip to Bryson City, near the Cherokee Reservation. While there, I made friends with a boy who lived at the motel. There was a pool, but I had brought no swim suit. Granny was elated. She didn't want me in that pool. I could drown. The boy rounded me up one of his, two sizes too big, and Papa talked her into letting me swim. She was fit to be tied. Papa watched for awhile, and then told her to stop worrying; I could swim like a fish.

Later in the week during our mountain vacation, I wanted to take a helicopter ride, a twenty minute tour over and around the mountains. She would not hear of it. The copter might crash. Now, I was the one fit to be tied. I threw a tantrum, and could pout quite well too. Papa told her he would ride with me. It could crash just as easily with both of us on board, she said. I pouted and brooded until I parlayed the helicopter ride into a trip to Frontier Land, a miniature version of the Disneyland Frontier Land. There I met and had my photograph taken with Jerry Mathers, *Leave the Beaver*. On television he was this dorky little kid. In real life, he was then a young pimple faced teenager, much larger than me.

It was tough being in the care of my Granny growing up, but Papa would let me do almost anything. That's why I struggled so I suppose, seeing him go down right before my very eyes. I walked into the house but there would be little time to visit. I quickly had to load him in my car and hit the road before those people caught us there. I put Papa in the front seat and Granny in the back. We took the trip to nowhere, riding in the country for awhile, then up and down familiar streets on their side of town and even on the other side of town, North Main. We chatted with Papa, pointed out this and that, and eventually told him we would take him home. The ruse worked. He was back in his house, mission accomplished.

The Care Giver's Son

The next part of my chore was to stay there long enough to help Granny get him to bed. Sometimes he would not be cooperative. This time he was. It was approaching midnight before I arrived back home. My Friday had vanished. Oh well, I still had Saturday. My parents would be back on Sunday. How difficult could this caretaking really be? The hardest thing for me had been being with Papa when he didn't seem to know who I was, for the most part. He may have come around a little toward the end, but even then I'm not sure. He never called me by name. Come to think of it, we didn't really have a conversation. I hated this about his condition. Some people call it hardening of arteries. Call it what you want; I think it's an awful disease. Papa deserved better.

Most of my Saturday went well. I did what I wanted to do, but in the back of my mind, I dreaded the approach of the setting sun. This time I didn't wait for Granny to call. I decided to nip it in the bud and head over there and do my duty early. My wife, estranged from the family, didn't accompany me. I parked in the back this time and caught them by surprise, but the surprise was on me. Papa was already ranting about those people and how they were going to accuse him of breaking in their home. We slipped on Papa's hat and coat, gave him his cane and we were off once again, driving the demons away.

After about an hour this time, there had been no great improvement. We pulled up to his house and he refused to go inside. Change of plans, I would take him to my house to see if we could break the spell. We arrived at my house unannounced. My wife respected my grandparents and was very cordial and played along. I flipped on the television. Papa always loved the *Andy Griffith show*. The opening scene had kids playing in a back yard. Papa viewed the television screen as a window and thought they were just outside the house. Worst still, he thought they belonged to the people in our house and we needed to go before they returned.

I should have found a ballgame or a shoot-um up. Papa loved the Cubs and Braves, but sadly it wasn't baseball season. Maybe a shoot-um up, a western, would have been a bad idea anyway, given his reaction to the television. He may have thought those cowboys and Indians were real. That may have prompted us having to circle the wagons. Well, he was a dead eye with his shotgun, so I'm sure he would have felt at home, defending the women and the children. I'm not sure who had the more vivid imagination, Papa or me.

It was a short visit but effective. By the time we returned to Papa's house, he thought he was home. By the time we got him to bed, and Granny and I visited a little, it was well past midnight. Not to worry, Mama and Daddy

The Care Giver's Son

would be back tomorrow. My turn in the barrel was almost over, thank goodness. It defies logic why I think this way. I loved Papa and Granny. They had always taken care of me. I wasn't as good at returning the favor. I wasn't a kid any longer, and apparently I thought I had earned the right as an adult to do what I wanted, when I wanted to do it and on my terms. Life doesn't exactly work out that way, does it?

T. Allen Winn

Tribute, My Way

I had finally returned home. I didn't know the funeral arrangements yet and dreaded the thoughts all together. Papa was dead. It was beginning to sink in, as bad as I hated the fact. I was supposed to go back to Granny and Papa's house tomorrow. All sorts of family were expected to be dropping by. The predictable funeral frenzy was off and running. I hated every aspect of it. This was a time for sadness and remembrance, not the social event of the year. Sorry, I just don't get it.

It's wonderful to see friends and family, especially those you haven't seen in ages, but it just plan irks me that some folks tend to be funeral hawks. There's something badly wrong when mourners arrive and make tracks to the kitchen, filling their plate and gorging themselves. That's not paying their respect; it's feed their face with free food. No, not everyone is like that, but I'm a people watcher and sadly, I see this trait too often for my taste. Besides, eating food at a time like this is the furthest thing from my mind.

Mama wandered about among the many guests, doing her part, with her dad now gone. Seeing after Papa had consumed her for so long, what would she do now that he was gone? Oddly, I think she enjoyed taking care of him, or anybody as far as that goes. She should have been a nurse. Granny would fill the void

The Care Giver's Son

quickly enough. She was needy, not dependent, but she would guilt Mama into being there for her, a given. She had her unique way of pulling the apron strings. We recognized it for what it was and allowed her to do it. It wasn't evil and I'm not even sure it was intentional, but she was good at it just the same. A caregiver requires someone to take care of, so she and Mama would work it out perfectly.

I can often come off as cynical and even heartless, but I can't help it; I call them like I see them. Granny did what she did; she couldn't help it, either. Mama did her thing as well. That's the game they had played all their lives. It was their game, not mine, is all I'm saying. It was the relationship they had had since Mama's childhood. I was just too independent to fall in line. Neither Mama nor Daddy had ever been needy parents, nor had I been a needy child. Mama and I were only children, but we didn't necessarily share the same philosophy. I never really asked for anything, expected things to be given to me on a silver platter; but I think Mama made sure I didn't go without anything because she had.

Life had been tough in the mill village for Mama growing up. Granny had been sickly, but had held a job most of her life in the very same textile mill that had employed both my parents. Papa was more the entrepreneur, taking odd jobs, a painter most of his life. He hunted. He fished. He had a garden. He raised chickens, an occasional goat for food. He was a provider; they made do. Mama worked hard at home and had struggled to attend school. She had never graduated; her responsibilities at home had taken precedence. She began working in the mill to support the family. Neither Granny nor Papa put much emphasis on obtaining an education. Why would they? Neither had been schooled and they had survived without book learning.

The caregiver in training had not had much of a young social life. She had shared those stories with me many times. As for that textile mill, both parents were determined I would break from tradition and would never work in a textile mill. Many of my high school classmates worked either part time or summer jobs at Milliken, some even working for Daddy. When I mentioned doing the same, he quickly put his foot down. They wanted me to have a better life.

Odd, Abbeville was a mill town. I thought it was my birthright to follow in their footsteps. This wasn't up for discussion. I'd have to find work elsewhere. I eventually did, working two summers for the Little River Co-op, swinging a bush ax and pruning long stands of pine trees on those endless right-of-ways. It was tough work, but outside, and I wasn't cooped up inside the mill. It taught me the value of a dollar and the pride in earning my own way. Yes, I was an only child and could have

The Care Giver's Son

probably asked for most anything and have gotten it, but I didn't. I wasn't raised to feel entitled. I didn't want handouts, someone giving me something for nothing. I had been taught real values. Work hard and prosper. Watch your spending and never buy something you can't afford.

There was an endless string of hugs, pats on my head or shoulders, family and friends, some strangers, consoling me for my lost. I hated it. I just wanted to be left alone, allowed to deal with Papa's death on my terms, my way, eating and socializing wasn't part of my grief process. Doing the necessary evil and being present and supportive wasn't doing it for me. This frustrated Mama. She interpreted this as I didn't care. That was the furthest thing from the truth. Bad memories of other funerals began surfacing. I was sinking into a very dark abyss.

My earliest memory of a traumatic death and funeral are still vivid in my mind. I was very young when my Uncle Hub died. He had been married to my Dad's sister for a brief period, maybe a year, when he suffered a heart attack. He was another one of those larger than life figures in my world. I remember how I was covertly sneaked into his hospital room. When he died I was devastated. Same scenario, family and friends gathered, laughing and doing too much socializing for me. Many of my cousins were in town and none were close to Uncle

Hub like me. All that they wanted to do was have a great ole time, playing in the yard and doing what kids do.

Not me, I couldn't. This was my time to mourn a man I truly loved. I withdrew, hid in a closet in one of the back bedrooms and cried. I didn't require anyone to comfort me or understand my anguish. I just wanted to be alone until this was over. It was my way of dealing. I guess it sort of still is.

The next funeral visit in my mind, an uncle's brother passed away and I accompanied another grandmother, my dad's mom, an aunt and uncle to Adams Run, near Edisto, in the Charleston, South Carolina area. The summer heat and humidity along the Carolina coast in August is relentless; not ideal conditions for a graveside service. While standing just outside the graveside tent, voices sounded as if they were fading away; my vision went dark like a closing curtain. I clung to that tent pole with a death grip. My grandmother later explained that I had passed out. I had miraculously held onto that pole until regaining consciousness. Another bad memory, the grandkids being her pallbearers, something grandkids should never ever be asked to do; just too cruel.

Funerals and me, they just don't gee haw. Now I'm faced with the worst one of all time. Mama had cared for Papa to the very end, by his side when he took his last breath. I had avoided that scenario at all cost. She had no

The Care Giver's Son

regrets for her decision, nor did I for mine. The difference, I understood and respected her for doing what she felt compelled to do, but she didn't understand nor support my decision to not be there. It was water under the bridge as far as I was concerned. I did it and would do it again. It's probably stupid to say what you won't do. I had said I would never marry again, but I did. Eating crow is an acquired taste.

So, just how was I going to handle this, Papa's death and the pending funeral? I did what I knew how to do. I slipped away into the front room, the mill house's living room, and closed the door. There I thought and complied my feelings. I'm not the best at articulating my feelings verbally. Too often my words are misconstrued or twisted; my deep voice sometimes portrays me in a different light. People think I'm mad when I'm not. My sarcasm certainly doesn't help my cause. I have a skewed sense of humor and my wit can be misunderstood or it prompts people to peg me as smart-alecky. I am wrongfully gifted.

I've always been much better at putting my feelings on paper. Writing, since an early age, has been a bit of an escape for me. Regardless of what most people think, I do possess a moral compass. Mine just often comes with a vivid imagination. No, I don't maintain a diary or journal, and I don't sit around writing a lot, but I do have my moments. Papa's death spurred one of those moments. I wrote to remember, to release my feelings and heal my hurt. It wasn't necessarily for anyone else's eyes. It was for me. I rarely ever shared what I had written with anyone.

There had been a few times as a child or young adult when my scribbling came back to bite me. I was just way too creative for my own good, I suppose. Most didn't understand my writing style. Heck, I didn't even know I had a unique writing style back then. I just wrote what I felt, what I envisioned, what I imagined. It flowed naturally when I did decide to write my thoughts down with a pad and pencil. Some were pure fantasy land, imaginary characters, evil versus good; then other times it was my inner most feelings.

I must have been a pre-teenager when I had written my very first story, possibly of novel proportions, now that I look back. My tools were a lead pencil and one of those paper sized school binders. I didn't know genre back then, but looking back, I suppose mine had been a cross between science fiction, fantasy with a smidgen of erotica tossed in. At eleven or twelve years old, I wasn't exactly an expert on sex, but that's why they call it fantasy. My story, while incomplete, must have spanned fifty or so pages. I wrote it primarily for me, but had shared it with a cousin my age.

Mama had apparently found it where I had it stashed in my room. Parents can be such snoops. What part of private don't they

The Care Giver's Son

understand? Do kids have no rights in this country? At a family gathering, they thought it would be the thing to do to read excerpts from MY STORY, without my permission. A much older cousin read it out loud and, of course, they had picked sections with the sexual undertones. Everyone laughed and thought it was funny. I snatched it from her hands and stormed from the room. Parents have a twisted sense of humor. I never completed that story. I destroyed it instead. Nobody would ever read it nor embarrass me again. Where was the caregiver when I needed her support? She showed no compassion towards me. I suppose you had to be sick or dying for her to kick into that mode. Believe me, I felt like crawling into a hole and dying.

The second most memorable moment in my young writing career occurred in high school. My English class was given the assignment of writing a short story. I couldn't wait. This would be my moment to shine; finally something I was good at, or at least that's how I spun it. I wrote a tale of a chess master passing though a small hick town in the middle of boondocks America. I played a lot of chess back then, so I fed off my passion for the board game. I penned a wonderful plot, so I thought.

My story was simple, but had a defining ending. The chess master was stranded in the tiny town, met a ten year old boy hanging out at the local country store, playing checkers as the pastime. He decided to use that checker board and teach the kid how to play the game of chess. After he was convinced the kid understood the moves of the various chess pieces and the concept, he played one last game with him before he departed. The kid ended up beating him in four moves, checkmate. The master never saw it coming, not expecting the kid to catch on so quickly. Now, that was a spectacular short story, worthy of an A.

I was proud of my accomplishment until I received my grade, an F. I couldn't believe it. I was crushed. The teacher had flunked me on grammar. She hadn't gotten it at all. I had purposely misspelled words in the boy's portion of the dialogue, to make him sound like an ole backwoods' hillbilly. I was devastated, demoralized, and damaged goods from a writing perspective. Back then you didn't argue with a teacher. Besides, I was too introverted to even try. My technique of writing was apparently ahead of its time. It would be a long span in my life before I'd write anything serious again. This incident had inflicted major injuries on my writing ego. I wasn't willing to swing at that third strike. I cried uncle and gave up instead. I bet she'd never make a good caregiver. She had lacked compassion.

Papa was dead. I had reached a crossroad. I had almost been banished from Mama–land for being uncaring, inconsiderate, and not supportive enough in the family's time of need.

The Care Giver's Son

I did the only thing I knew how to do. This was one of those reach deeply and cleanse my mortal soul moments. It had nothing to do with any regrets for not doing my part, being a better caregiver, nor guilt for not being there when he had passed, and I was certainly not wallowing in a pity party. This was for me, nobody else. I would not make the same mistake, share with others, and undergo their scrutiny and critiquing. In the end, my heart, my inner most feelings had produced a simple poem.

I may have just run my own stop sign, ignored my own advice, and taken a swing at strike three. I shared my poem with a friend, a close confidant and she encouraged me to share it with family. If it had come from anyone but her, I would have probably passed on the situation, but I trusted her opinion. We assembled a very small audience and I allowed her to read it. I couldn't. My heart would only unleash a gully washer from my tear ducts if I tried. She began reading...

MY PAPA
He was my Papa
I was his only grandson.
The love we shared for each other;
Made our hearts more like one.

His mouth didn't hold any teeth.
His head didn't have much hair.
But his heart had it all.

T. Allen Winn

God's lucky to have him up there.

He taught me about that garden.
How to plant those rows so straight.
The first time I planted my own,
I could tell he thought it was great.

In the woods he was at his best.
All squirrels and rabbits would run.
When it came to making a shot,
His ability compared to none.

When it was time to go fishing,
No one loved it more.
Whether it was cats, brim or crappie,
The fishing was never poor.

Papa never met a stranger.
To everyone he was Uncle John.
He especially loved all children
And they loved their Uncle John.

He really loved his Ruby.
He cherished his Mary too.
Thomas was the son her never had.
For him, there was nothing they
wouldn't do.

I'm going to miss my Papa.
For me, losing him is a real test.
But I know he's there with God.
For us, we shared the best.

The Care Giver's Son

When she finished, there was not a dry eye in the room. My words were simple, a grandson's love for his Papa, and it left no doubt how I felt. I aired the laundry for everyone to see inside my heart. I had made a major breakthrough, and I think, even the caregiver got it, why this had been so difficult for me. We all deal with things differently and shouldn't be judged for our differences. Comparing me to someone I'm not or stereotyping me isn't going to work. I'm too rebellious and unique to ever follow your chosen path for me. Let me be me and it'll work out in the long run. You're fighting a losing battle if you think you can change me or mold me into an image that fits your needs. In the words of Popeye, *I yam what I yam*.

A suggestion was made that my simple poem should be included in the epitaph that would be handed out during Papa's funeral. I reluctantly agreed. Then dropped the other shoe; would I read it as part of the eulogy at the Pentecostal Church, in front of those attending Papa's funeral. There is where I drew the line. I would never make it through the reading. This was more to me than just a poem. I compromised, granting the pastor the honor. Now came the next roughest thing in my life; going to the funeral home to receive friends, and of all things, an open viewing of Papa's body lying in the casket. I wasn't ready for that, far from it.

T. Allen Winn

Being Sociable, while Kicking And Screaming

Fretfulness and procrastination are not very flattering attributes, especially if worn and displayed simultaneously. I so dreaded going to the meet and greet family gathering. This is so against what I believe. I'd never be on the 'A List' for a wake. How could I pattern this to suit my agenda, my last tribute to Papa? That was the million dollar question. Perhaps if I could leap that hurdle, I could make this work. Viewing his body, anyone's body, just seems so bizarre. Why can't people just settle for picturing a wonderful image of the deceased, and not a body ravaged by prolonged illness? It's too much like gawking; nothing respectiveful about it, I'm just saying; Mama's words too.

I mustered up the courage to do the needful, the jobless caregiver prodding me along. I really should cut Mama some slack. This wasn't her cup of tea either. Fortunately, the immediate family gathers at the funeral home first, to pay their respect before the circus begins. Still, I didn't embrace being the first in line, but I had come to terms with it, and knew what needed to be done. I filed in behind Granny, Mama and Daddy, taking my turn in the pecking order, viewing Papa one last time.

The Care Giver's Son

A lump the size of one of those chunks of coal was caught in my throat. I could sure use that handmade poker to force feed it back down. Taking the largest breath of my life, I leaned over and touched Papa on his hand, before pinning an Atlanta Braves' loyal fan pin to his lapel. He dearly loved the Braves. I then placed a 4-10 shot gun shell in his pocket, telling him he might need it to bag a rabbit or a squirrel. With that simple ceremony, my heart had been lifted. I was ready to let him go. As always, I had to do it my way. Never once did the thought cross my mind, he looked at peace, so natural looking or just like Papa. He was **MY PAPA** and always will be. Now I could face the line of folks here to pay their last respects; not because I wanted to, but because it was the right thing to do.

As a family, we muddled through the formalities. Papa was finally laid to rest. It was funny in the days to follow how Granny began watching the Atlanta Braves. She never cared for them while Papa was alive, but for whatever reason, she had embraced the antics of Chipper Jones and his other teammates. Possibly this made her feel close to Papa, who knows? It was funny somehow she was under the impression that Andrew Jones, another one of the outfielders, was Chipper Jones' son. First of all, they were about the same age and secondly, they were of different nationalities. I never did understand where she got that notion. She embraced the Braves, but only when the Braves regular announcers were calling the game. She didn't care for any of the other network commentators. Papa would have been proud and I'm sure is smiling down on her.

Before Papa passed away, Mama or Granny would switch on the game, hoping to occupy his time. Papa would use his cane mimicking swinging at the ball, envisioning the television as his private portal, including him in the ballpark as a participant. He'd even try to catch and throw the ball. We had to laugh about that sort of thing. His cane became a putter when watching the PGA. There's no telling how many holes he actually birdied. Yep, that cane had more uses than a Swiss knife.

Mama fell back into a life of normalcy; or at least as normal as Granny would allow. Granny had this gift of being able to guilt Mama into staying on a short leash. She had manipulated Mama since her childhood. She could come down with a severe case of melancholy if she sensed Mama was drifting out of reach of her apron strings. The caregiver, with a minor reprieve, had one weekly outlet that provided her relief from what life tossed at her. She so enjoyed those Saturday night dances at the Anderson VFM. An assortment of family and friends would pile into their travel van and make the thirty mile trip. There, Mama would sip a little adult beverage and could dance and

The Care Giver's Son

forget her troubles. Everyone deserves a little downtime.

I don't think Mama ever lied about where she was on those Saturday nights but, even as a woman nearly sixty years old, she didn't do certain things in front of Granny. Dancing and drinking were taboo, so she kept those her little secrets. I must clarify. Mama was not a drinker, but she would have a few to loosen up her feet and chase away her inhibitions on Saturday nights; no harm, no foul. Some things were best not disclosed to Granny though. It wouldn't be worth the grief.

Granny didn't require 24/7 care at this point in her life, but she was needy just the same. She had her driver's license so she could get about, typically just taking short trips to the grocery or visiting family or friends just minutes away She did attend Wednesday night prayer meetings and Sunday church at the local Pentecostal Church, just a couple of blocks away. Funny, she had only gotten her driver's license in 1969, the same year she bought her first automobile, a four door, blue, Chevrolet Impala. Granny was in her mid fifties when she made that purchase at the local dealership. She remembered her car arriving in town by train.

Granny was very independent in a lot of ways, but when she wanted her way, she would have one of those nervous spells, as she called them. I'm not saying these spells were intentional, but they sure did seem to be convenient. She could worry up one of those spells with the snap of a finger. This typically resulted in Mama having to cancel her plans and be there with Granny. Saturday nights were becoming routine for one of her little episodes. Granny, the saint, did have an agenda. She'd pull the same thing on me from time to time if I was available for such an occasion. One had to feel responsible to act responsibly. I could somehow justify my actions and my busy life style and leave the adult babysitting to Mama and Daddy. Thank goodness, they had more supportive family and friends and that sort of eased me off the hook.

Emotionally, I was just not cut out for all this neediness and the commitment it requires. No one said self justification was a pretty thing, nor excusable. Looking the other way, until asked specifically to step up to the plate, tended to better suit my demeanor and lifestyle. I don't know what made me think and act like this. I'm sure that clinical studies exist that explain my behavior. If I had really thought I was doing something wrong, I could have sought a cure for my inadequacies. Admitting you have a problem is the first step, right. I had not reached that breakthrough moment yet. I still had the ultimate caregiver as my crutch. She embraced her role, or so it seemed to me. Why deny Mama, her calling. Step aside and let her do her thing, I'm just saying.

The Care Giver's Son

A double whammy loomed in the not too foreseeable future. As the saying goes, enjoy while you can. That was never too difficult for me. I took very few prisoners in my quest in the search of the perfect life, to enjoy with reckless abandon was my creed. I have the scars to prove it, as do my parents. I don't consider myself a bad person, but I have certainly made my fair share of bad decisions. With those worst of the worst, I have maximized the art of burning and crashing with vigor. I've never halfway done anything, good or bad. I have this knack for taking it to the limit, jumping the canyon or driving off the cliff, very little wiggle room in between. The consequences aren't always pretty. I'm an only child but I can deliver the misery of three when I set my mind to it. It's another one of many invaluable attributes.

I'm fortunate that Mama has never had to be my caregiver to date. It's not because of any lack of delivering on my part. I've dodged my fair share of bullets, and caused a bus load of stressful moments for my parents. I'm not sure why I thrive on living on the edge, taking too many risks, doing stuff I absolutely should not be doing. Again, I'm sure there is a clinical study to diagnose this behavior too. It's almost as if I have a self destructive mode, nine lives maybe. Could there ever be a life lesson ahead for me, or would I just keep flipping over the hour glass?

T. Allen Winn

Life is What You Make It, or Not

My world picked up where it had left off, spinning along, no major distractions or illnesses, with my tiny circle of family seemingly healthy and back on track. This didn't mean that Granny wouldn't have more of those nervous spells, especially now, living alone for the very first time, but at least it wasn't a daily event. Mama stopped after work before going home. The mill was no more than three blocks from Granny's house. If Daddy wasn't playing golf or taking care of his household and yard chores, he checked in on her. I kept in touch, sort of, when it was convenient for me. Storm clouds were brewing. The not so distant future would be less sunny and cheerful.

Daddy had taken over the yard maintenance for Granny when Papa's heath had failed. It wasn't a very large yard. I had mowed it weekly as a kid, earning a buck fifty each time I had. I could have done it now for free but allowed Daddy to do it. He was after all retired and I was still working. It seemed the logical thing for him to do, at least from my perspective. I had a large yard to maintain. He probably needed tasks to occupy his time. This didn't come without terrible circumstances, at least not from Granny's side of the fence.

A hedgerow ran the full width of Granny's front yard. It periodically required trimming, as

The Care Giver's Son

did an assortment of ornamental shrubs scattered about her lot. Granny had a green thumb and could grow almost anything. She could root sprouts from the parent plants, seldom having to ever buy new ones. Her pride and joy was her huge flowering snowball bush in the right front corner of her yard. Seasonally it had enormous blooming clusters, and that season was now.

Daddy, after trimming the hedges, figured he may as well prune the shrubbery. This seemed to be the logical thing to do while he had the equipment available. Using electric trimmers on bushes is sort of like giving someone a haircut. A barber takes a little off the top and evens the sides. Barbers are professionals and can do this flawlessly. Unfortunately, Daddy wasn't a barber, and a nip here and there can get out of hand, especially when you're using electric trimmers and not manual pruning shears. He was not accustomed to using them so things went bad. A blooming snowball bush, measuring over six feet wide and six feet high, was transformed into a series of leafless sticks no more than two feet high. Daddy called this pruning back the shrubs. He was accustomed to pruning evergreen bushes, what a mess?

Granny was devastated by the end result. I'm not sure how she avoided one of those nervous spells. While Granny was next to tears with Mama, she never let on to Daddy just how traumatized she really was. She would never hurt his feelings. He is a good man with good intentions, she would say, and he had gone the extra mile with Papa's illness. It would eventually grow back. Sadly, that old bush never regained its beauty. It almost seemed to have been permanently stunted by the trimming event. Unbeknownst to us, this could have been a sign, if we had been looking for one.

Mama, jealous I think of Daddy being retired, had come to the conclusion that she should retire too. Daddy had taken early retirement so, if it was good for the goose, it should be good for the gander. They assessed their financial situation and it seemed sound enough for her to do so. Hindsight, this would be a blessing in disguise, possibly a premonition for her to enjoy life with him at this specific time. Either way, things do happen for a reason, our destiny is chosen, good, bad or ugly.

It's always a dice roll, trying to choose that moment in time to retire. Some folks wait until their health has begun to decline, and then they can't enjoy it as they had envisioned. Others, because their job doesn't stress them, work until a ripe old age. Some can't retire because they haven't prepared for it. One's financial stability and ability to afford insurance, often weighs in heavily. Other factors impact the choice to take the plunge. Will you stay active or become a couch potato? For some, if not handled properly, this can be a death sentence, both physically and emotionally. Most jobs are a form of social activity, interacting with people for whatever reason. Making that transition to a home life without a plan can have disastrous results. Unfortunately we have no real control over the final outcome, our destiny.

The recovering caregiver certainly deserved some downtime, an opportunity to enjoy the fruits of her labor. She and Daddy had worked hard, as do most people, to reach this stage in their lives. Life in a textile mill can wear a person down. They had fared better than most, and had invested wisely to prepare them for this chapter in their lives. It became a running joke between me and them, for them not to squander my inheritance. In reality, I hoped they spent every single penny and did all the things they had always wanted to do. Nothing would make me happier than to see them happy. I have never been one to dwell on money or material things. I pay my bills and live for the moment. My method to my madness has served me well.

They both loved to travel, especially ocean cruises. They booked one as soon as possible, and had their own little group that typically traveled together. The destination wasn't really that important. Mama and Daddy weren't into visiting the islands or taking excursions. They were perfectly content to live the celebrity life, the ship their hotel, and allow the crew to wait on them hand and foot. The cruise was perfect for their lifestyle with the all inclusive meals, entertainment and cabin services. This was their ultimate vacation, leaving the driving to the captain. It didn't get any better than this for them, I'm saying.

Over the next couple of years, their retirement went well for the most part. Every journey has potholes in the road, those little curves you never see coming, but they made do, as Mama would often say. My folks were survivors and adapted when the situation called for it. Granny would have her occasional nervous spells, some severe enough to land her in the emergency room or hospital, but she always bounced back. Daddy continued to play golf at least a couple of times a week with his cronies, at a nine hole golf course, High Meadows. He was never that good at it, but did it really matter as long as he enjoyed the fellowship?

Almost daily they checked on Granny and the Sunday dinner tradition continued, sometimes at her house, other times at Mama and Daddy's. I wasn't a regular participant. I marched to my own drummer, but regardless, the band played on without me. I continued to be drafted for Granny duty when my folks were traveling. At least this didn't require riding her around to escape those people, and I didn't have to tuck her into bed each night. She was of

The Care Giver's Son

sound mind and fairly independent. She did not, however, like my folks going off on cruises. They would wait until the last possible moment to spring it on her. I believe they did this to avoid one of those premeditated nervous spells.

My moment had arrived; a seven day cruise had been scheduled. I would be reporting for duty on Saturday when they departed for Bermuda. I had grown up accustomed to long vacations and travel with my folks. Almost every other year we ventured to Daytona, Florida, for two weeks. Daddy loved car racing so the vacations were scheduled around the Fourth of July, to take in the Daytona 500 and all the activities associated with the race. When not heading to Florida, we had taken other one to two week long trips across our great country. I had gotten to see much of our fine land at an early age but I had never been on a cruise. They had begun cruising after I had flown the nest.

After they departed, I did my best to substitute for Mama. It was to my advantage that she could not critique me from her ocean oasis. Granny appeared to be on her best behavior, making my task a breeze. This did come with fringe benefits. She so enjoyed feeding my face with all sorts of my favorites. A few extra pounds of baggage would be in store for me over the next seven days. Granny enjoyed doing it, so who am I to deny her the satisfaction and gratification. I'm a team player, or can be. Caregiving under the right circumstances isn't half bad. Well, I suppose it really isn't technically termed caregiving, if that person can do for themselves.

The week passed rather uneventfully, other than me transitioning to her requirements and dismissing mine. It hadn't really been that difficult, and the stress level had not been intense, unlike dealing with Papa's illness. Granny still looked and acted like Granny, and for that I was immensely thankful. Oddly, I had enjoyed my time with Granny. Maybe I was coming around just a tad, or possibly it was the lesser of two evils, my home life not being a bowl of cherries of late. Dirty laundry should remain where it belongs, and in the dirty clothes basket, so hush my mouth, so to speak.

The Bermuda cruise, while enjoyable, had revealed something quite disturbing to Mama. She shared her concern about Daddy with me. He had kept to himself much of the time, avoiding people, almost detached from the crowd. He'd wander off alone instead of hanging out with the rest. Even more puzzling, he tended to be lethargic, lacking the normal pep in his step. He dragged behind, something that was not normal for him. Daddy usually knew but one speed, wide open. Mama couldn't quite put her finger on it but something had changed. When asked, he gave no real explanation and simply shrugged it off.

The Care Giver's Son

She moved on to the fun stuff and told me about the incredible entertainment, amazing food, and the impeccable service. She had been treated like a queen, and loved every minute of it. One of the more humorous moments had occurred when she had experienced an awkward moment in their cabin. She, Daddy and a family friend, ex-sister in-law, were roomies. Daddy had given the girls some breathing room to pretty up for the evening's festivities, and had exited the premises. Mama had just popped out of the shower, naked as the day she was born, when room service arrived. She hid behind the cabin door while her cabin mate answered the door and retrieved the beverage tray, taking her time, tipping and so forth.

Mama had forgotten one important detail in her little hide and seek counter measure; a full length mirror was mounted on the opposite wall from the cabin door. While she huddled behind the door, she remained in full view for Pablo's eyes only. The cabin steward never flinched, smiled or closed his eyes. Possibly he had seen these sights before, or he was an accomplished Peeping Tom. The caregiver had been caught literally with her pants down, and then some. From then on, when she saw the little cabin steward, she'd never know if he was undressing her with his eyes. Why bother really, he had seen the goods, so no imagination was required.

It just gave new meaning to his complementary smile.

Granny, safely returned to her hands, I focused my attention back on my life. Daddy's situation didn't improve after their return. He still moved about like a turtle, said Mama. He didn't appear focused on his yard work, and golf didn't seem to be a priority, although he did go. Little things continued to pile up; Daddy just wasn't acting right. Mama is not a firm believer in going to the doctor, unless she's cornered and she has exhausted all the home remedies, but she couldn't diagnose Daddy's problem nor come up with a treatment or cure. She finally bit the bullet and encouraged him to see a doctor. Encouragement, by Mama's standards, means you're going to see a doctor, not up for debate. Daddy never bucked her, followed her wishes. He knew better. Besides, he was never one to argue about anything.

Test indicated he had suffered a silent heart attack, still yet another new medical term. Why was it that no one in our family was ever stricken with something simple, one we had heard of before, not all the mumbo jumbo that would require further explanation. We bit, what was a silent heart attack and just what did it mean for Daddy's well being?

The doctor explained no heart attack was a good heart attack. Silent heart attacks often could be the more deadly. He explained that

The Care Giver's Son

there were several reasons why some people have heart attacks without apparent symptoms. Some people have high pain thresholds, or a high tolerance for pain. They simply don't notice or realize what others would find difficult to ignore. Some medical conditions, such as diabetes, blunt the nerves that carry pain impulses. No, he confirmed, Daddy was not diabetic. Other people just ignore the symptoms and are very good at shrugging it off. Lastly, the lack of blood flow to the heart, cardiac ischemia, simply does not produce chest pain.

After the doctor talked with Daddy and Mama, he leaned more towards the cardiac ischemia theory. With this, victims might experience a shortness of breath or transient weakness. Bingo, it explained his sluggishness and general lack of motivation. Because these silent heart attacks don't produce the symptoms of a normal heart attack, they are often not detected until long after the fact, after the damage has been done, he explained. An electrocardiogram had detected the weakness in Daddy's heart. He wanted to admit Daddy to Providence Heart & Vascular Institute in Columbia for further examination and determine the necessary treatment.

Mama hated hospitals, almost as much as she despised funerals. One thing for sure, this was not an option. Furthermore, without proper diagnosis and follow-up, a funeral could be in her future, Daddy's. She recruited the assistance of her favorite ex-sister-in-law and soon the two of them, with Daddy in tow, headed to Providence, just under a two hour drive away. Mama had kicked into gear, the caregiver switch activated. I was promoted once again to Granny duty. It was odd, Daddy for the most part, looked healthy, so it was hard to fathom he had suffered a heart attack. Of course, I had not witnessed firsthand the behavior Mama had observed, so I'd just have to take everyone's word.

Things turned ugly after they reamed out Daddy's partially blocked arteries. Like Mama, he had hardly ever visited a doctor and had never been on any medication. Being hospitalized and now medicated slammed him both mentally and physically. This stay marked the beginning of the wild roller coaster ride ahead, one that none of us were prepared to ride, and I like roller coasters.

The first night after opening his arteries, he had an extremely terrible reaction to the medication. This transformed Daddy into a legitimate and certified wild man. I received the phone call from a family friend that I needed to make the hour and half drive to help Mama with him. Relieved of Granny duty, I now had a more challenging adventure awaiting me, baptism by fire!

Leaving work, the family friend and I headed to the hospital. Upon arrival, Mama

The Care Giver's Son

filled us in on the details. Daddy had completely lost it during the night, pulling out his IV, bloodying up the sheets and floor before a nurse walked in to discover the horror movie scene.

The friend spent the second night with Mama while I pulled the midnight Daddy shift. Neither of us slept. Daddy stayed alert and I had to constantly persuade him that staying in the hospital one more night was very important. So far he hadn't tried to jerk out his IV, he watched me intently and I kept a vigil on him. I just hoped we survived the night uneventfully. This wasn't my cup of tea for sure. Mama was the caregiver, not me. They released him the next day.

Seeing Daddy in that hospital bed brought back a rush of flashbacks. I thought about Papa and I hadn't really thought about him in forever. Daddy had survived a heart attack, and he had experienced some sort of wild reaction to the medication they had administered. Was I about to lose him too? It was just me and Daddy, now, sitting in this room, confined and neither of us wanted to be here, especially him.

I was on night watch, making sure he didn't go berserk like he had done last night. I had no experience in dealing with this. We're surrounded by professionals who should be doing something, not me. Their solution to his actions, strap him in his bed like some loony, some bedside manner. They gave him the medicine that prompted him to do what he had done last night. He would have never reacted as he did, if they hadn't. I must admit, this was becoming a little too creepy.

I sat in a side chair watching him watch me. It reminded me of one of those stare down competitions, who would be the first to blink? Daddy had never been a man for conversation. The fruit doesn't fall for from the tree. I'm moody that way also. Neither of us possessed Mama's gift of gab. She was more like a rapid firing machine. Mama could ask you three questions before you answered the first, and she didn't mind asking. She said that was the only way you learned anything, by asking. A wealth of knowledge should ooze from her pores then. I hoped she was asking these doctors all the right questions.

With so little talking, it opened the door for way too much thinking. I'm an excellent thinker. Unfortunately, bad times haunted my thoughts. I couldn't switch the brain off those Papa memories, his last days, hours, and me avoiding the inevitable. Now here I am in what could be a similar situation. Just what would I do if the worst case scenario happened right here and now? Daddy seemed healthy enough, other than him being perched in that hospital bed with all the contraptions monitoring his vitals. Vitals, just the mere thought of that word sent chills down my spine and rang way too seriously in my brain. Nope, I'm not a doctor or

The Care Giver's Son

a nurse and I'm the least likely candidate for caregiver duty. I was much better suited for Granny watch. Here, I was out of my element. My safety net, professionals were a buzz away.

I asked Daddy did he need anything. He didn't. He seemed oddly detached, acting nothing like the Daddy I knew. I suppose if I had suffered a heart attack and that bizarre episode last night, found myself still in the hospital with my future yet to be determined, I could act a little squirrelly too. After last night's bloody event, I was almost fearful to turn my back on him. Mama would never forgive me if I flunked in my caregiving duties by allowing a repeat performance. Watching Daddy keep a watchful eye on me made me think he might just be waiting for another opportunity. Possibly he had formulated an escape plan and was just waiting for the right moment to implement it. This was the cat playing the mouse, me.

I needed to think happy thoughts, not easy in a hospital room. My mind drifted from one subject to another, perusing the files stored away in my memory bank. I couldn't shake thinking about Papa, and I'm sure it was because I feared a repeat with Daddy, losing another loved one. Gloom and doom weighed me down. I'm the last person a sick patient needs around for moral support and boosting their mood, that's for sure. I absolutely didn't want to be here if anything happened to the man in that hospital bed on my watch.

Assumptions are a crap shoot at best, but I figured sooner or later Daddy would succumb to sleep, especially after last night's events. He must surely be suffering from fatigue, plus they would probably administer something to make him rest. Happy thoughts, I really need happy thoughts. I pictured Papa in those Camel overalls, the Papa before the sickness brought him down. Those good ole Papa hunting and fishing stories usually cheered me up. He could surely put himself in the middle of some comical situations, usually not intentionally. Daddy had that gift too. I wish Papa would have been here this very minute. He could have broken the ice and had us in stitches, and that's a fact.

After his death, one of my cousins shared a little story about Papa that I had never heard. I thought I would share it with Daddy and lighten the mood. As the episode goes, Papa was at a Wednesday night prayer meeting at the Pentecostal Holiness Church, and Granny as always, was nudging him to keep him awake and prevent him from snoring. The preacher apparently was giving the congregation tips on how to avoid going to Hell and directed them along the righteous path to Heaven. He held up the good book, the Bible, and waved it about, making sure he had gotten everyone's attention, even Papa's, thanks to Granny's persistence.

The Care Giver's Son

The preacher issued a serious warning to his gathered flock. It was the responsibility for each and every one of them to take time and read the scripture. To be blunt and elevate the awareness and implications of not doing this, he warned them that if they failed to read the Bible, it could take them down the wrong fork in the road, and a sure path to Hell. He asked for a show of hands for those who took time to read the Bible as often as they could. Papa didn't raise his hand, but instead he stood up and addressed the preacher.

"Brother John, do you have something to add."

"Yes sir, I do, Preacher. I reckon I'm going to be one of those to burn in Hell.'

Granny looked at him in shock. She couldn't believe the words spewing from Papa's mouth.

"Yes sir, I'm going to burn in Hell, because I can't read a lick."

My cousin said that comment brought the house down, everyone laughing and clapping at Papa's honesty. The preacher had to scramble for a response to Papa's revelation, not expecting his sermon to take such an eventful turn for the worse. He quickly reassured Papa that the Lord would make exceptions for those unable to read, noting that listening to the scripture would obviously give him a pass. This would have been one of those moments tailor made for filming. It could have been worthy of the grand prize on that funniest home video show. I wish I would have been there.

The story did lighten the mood and stir a little laugh from Daddy. Mission accomplished, for both of us. The power of healing had been delivered by a Papa moment. Maybe I was onto something. Comic relief may be what we both needed to chase away the demons looming on the fringes of our sanity. I had to keep them coming, but I had no rehearsed stand up routine. I decided to stick to the script as long as I could, and dig up more Papa stories.

There was the time Papa took me hunting and allowed me to have a gun for the very first time. Up until then, I had only accompanied him and helped him spot the squirrels. He had decided it was time for me to be armed and dangerous. He didn't tell Granny. Smart move on his part, because it would have only fretted her into one of those nervous spells. I think I was nine or ten. Hunting squirrels is about as bad as going fishing. It's a waiting game, just like watching that cork bobbing in the water.

I recapped the hunt out at Mister Powell's. Even if he had heard it, it was better than nothing. Just off the left of Mister Powell's house was a deep and long hollow. Papa said it was loaded with acorns and hickory nut trees. The hunting plan was always the same. Stake out a spot on the hill and wait for the squirrels to begin showing their furry faces. The only difference this time, Papa would take me to a spot, safely out of gunshot range, and have me wait for them to arrive. He moved further up the hollow and staked out his honey hole.

Daddy listened intently, no change in expression on his somber face, so I continued. Papa had equipped me with his extra 4-10 single barrel shot gun, one that had previously belonged to his deceased brother, Uncle Joe. Just like being in this hospital room, waiting for squirrels gives you too much time to think. My imagination ran wild and with it came the fidgets. You're supposed to be as quiet and still as possible, not necessarily the best trait for a ten year old boy, alone in the woods, with a gun, on the side of hill. Remember what Elmer Fudd says, '*Be very, very quiet, we're hunting wabbits.*' In this case, replace his warning with squirrels, I told him.

I didn't wear or own a watch, so how much time actually went by while I waited is anyone's guess, but it sure seemed like an eternity to me. Then I heard it, that unmistakable rustle of leaves, the sound I had heard many times before, when Papa had shushed me and had told me to listen. A squirrel was somewhere on the ground below me, digging about for nuts. I readied my weapon just as Papa had trained me. My breathing was labored and my heart felt as if it would burst through my chest. I regretted saying that part to Daddy, given his heart situation. He didn't flinch so maybe it hadn't bothered him. He was still watching me.

The rustling of leaves grew louder, the sound drew closer. The little grey squirrel hopped into view. It's funny. You think about rabbits hopping, but squirrels actually move about in short hops too. So what did I do? I yelled, "There he is." What a stupid thing to do, then I fired the shotgun. I must have killed my limit in leaves. My quarry would live to forage another day. Daddy did laugh, so my form of therapy was working for both of us. Continuing, Papa showed up a few minutes later, beaming with delight. Unlike the happy catfish story, I was empty handed this time, and had not bagged my very first squirrel. Papa eased my ego, telling me there would be more opportunities. I hoped Daddy and I would have the same opportunities, to do stuff together, make memories.

I reminisced, reminding Daddy how Papa could skin those critters and then Granny would either fry them up or make squirrel dumplings. It made my lips smack thinking about it. Daddy would occasionally ask me the time. Other than that, he remained quiet for the most part, and wide awake. The time had eventually pushed well beyond midnight and still he sat, looking about, saying very little. I was fearful to catch a catnap, unsure what he might do if he had the chance. I thought about Papa and how he was the master of escape, even though these were

The Care Giver's Son

entirely different circumstances. Daddy didn't suffer from dementia or hardening of the arteries, but there was something in those eyes; something that made me oh so weary and concerned.

I wished Daddy would have been able to talk about what he had felt. It would have probably done us both some good. Neither one of us was as accomplished at it as Mama, so we seemed content to just try to muddle our way through the night. It had been forever since I pulled an all-nighter, but this was more like a standoff. Daddy wasn't giving into sleep and I couldn't, not as long as he didn't. If I did, I better keep one eye open, just in case. Nurses checked on him every couple of hours, so I'm not sure how he would have been able to sleep, even if he had wanted to.

Imagining the visions of his bloody fiasco from the previous night presented just enough edginess to prevent me from dropping my guard. Sure, I'd head-bob occasionally, but would snap back to attention. Each time Daddy would be staring at me but saying nothing. It gave me the impression of a prisoner just biding his time for that one chance to escape. I really resented having to view Daddy in this light, feeling I indeed played the part of a prison guard. Instead of a caregiver, I was the designated gatekeeper. I was no more comfortable in this role than I had been in the other. I wasn't cut out for this. It was way above my pay grade. Time snailed along.

Somehow we made it to morning. He never slept, nor did I. What was next, I wondered. When would they allow him to go home? I just wanted him to be Daddy again, and for all this other crap to just go away. Is that too much to ask? Maybe it's just a bit selfish on my part, wishing my world would return to normal. There's caring and there's caregiving. I obviously lacked in that giving part. I had reported for duty and completed my shift, and now waited for further instructions. I'm sure more marching orders were in my future. Mama would be the bearer of those instructions, without a doubt. Care Bear would be on top of her game, hitting the floor running. There's safety in numbers, but nowhere to hide when you're an only child.

Over the next few years, the signs would be obvious for someone looking for them. We weren't. Daddy always had the knack, a gift, for doing really stupid and off the wall things, so that alone would have never raised a flag. Hey, I'm not calling my dad stupid, but he could be quite entertaining; ask anyone.

Daddy had always possessed energy beyond his years; unable to sit still. He no longer displayed that nervous energy, but we shrugged that off too, blaming his heart problem, plus being older and the addition of medication, something new in his life for sure. Daddy had

The Care Giver's Son

also given up smoking. He didn't seem to talk as much as he used to do, but he always had quiet spurts, so no big deal there either.

We can look back now and pick out key events, but what good does that really do us. I know you've probably noticed that I've been throwing that "we" word around a lot but I can include myself this time. It doesn't require my complete undivided attention and participation.

I still drew comfort from watching from the sidelines. I'm a bench warmer, remember. I'm totally comfortable with sitting on the bench and not playing in the big game. Late in the game, even bench warmers get a little playing time. I said that Daddy was undergoing changes, not me; not yet. This is his moment, not necessarily to shine.

During the couple of years after our scare with his heart problem, both now retired, they had gone on a couple of more cruises. I even accompanied them on one. They loved to travel and never passed up an opportunity.

Every Saturday they were out with friends dancing at the VFW or occasionally supporting the Shriners at functions. Daddy continued to play a little golf. My marriage ended and I started my year long separation living with my folks until my divorce became final. I would eventually remarry. Suddenly I came face to face with the daily grind, seeing what Mama endured. Even under their roof, I did only what I had to do. Old habits die hard. I had a long way to go and a short time to get there, Jerry Reed, Smokey and the Bandit, right?

So life appeared almost normal. Mama still took care of Granny or at least checked in on her daily. She still lived in her little mill house. Granny enjoyed her independence, but really missed Papa. We all did. Oh how the plot was about to thicken.

Never underestimate your problem or your ability to deal with it.
*-- **Robert H. Schuller***

The Care Giver's Son

Déjà Vu

Daddy began doing strange things, even for him. He'd forget where items were located, or misplaced others like his watch or wallet. All were just little episodes with him still flying under the radar. Mama just sort of put the blinders on and fussed at him when he made his little mistakes. Daddy just took what she dished out in stride. I hated listening to it. What difference did it really make? The man was absentminded, so what?

Staying with Daddy one weekend while Mama traveled out of town with my new bride to be, I did get a taste of Daddy's, how can I put it, odd behavior. Like I've mentioned, he has always given us plenty of ammunition to raze him about, so nothing normally surprises me; normally, but there's always a first time.

Now for the record, this man loved tomatoes. We had a dozen or so vine ripe ones that should typically last for a few days. He and I decided to have tomato sandwiches for our dinner. While I retrieved the bread and mayo from the refrigerator and poured us glasses of sweet tea, Daddy sliced the tomatoes.

I should have been paying a little better attention to him and his chore, because he sliced up at least half dozen tomatoes before I halted his progress. Like I said, he sure loved tomatoes.

I sat down at the kitchen table across from him, only to watch Daddy place the entire platter of tomatoes directly in front of him. He salted and peppered them, and then began eating directly from his sliced bounty. I sat there mouth gapped wide open, realizing he had no intention of sharing them with me or making any sandwiches.

Laughing it off, I peeled an extra tomato and made myself a couple of sandwiches. He in the meantime ate the entire platter. I told him I couldn't believe he had just done that and we both had quite the chuckle. I knew something was wrong with this picture, but like I've said, he has always kept us entertained with his antics.

While he didn't seem like his old self, no alarm bells sounded. I stayed with him until Mama and my wife to be returned. I recapped the tomato caper and we all laughed about it again, including Daddy.

Daddy often did stupid things long before this episode. I remember once seeing the riding lawn mower he was supposed to be riding, motoring across the yard without him. He had been knocked off by the neighbor's low window awning. Bleeding from a head wound, he ran frantically behind it and leapt back into the seat. He finished mowing the lawn before seeing about his head. Thankfully he wasn't severely hurt, because we did have a good laugh.

The Care Giver's Son

Then there was the time during one of their vacation trips, that Daddy had everyone in stitches. Like most men, me included, we have this magnetic pull towards the television remote. What's the first thing we do after we check into the motel room; yes, we grab that remote and surf. Daddy, supporting our legacy, grabbed the remote, mesmerized by that magical viewing box and he backed up slowly, intent on sitting on the bed. Instead he planted his butt on the floor between the two beds. Even he laughs every time that tale is told.

Then there is my all time favorite. Mama and I were already positioned at the kitchen table, breakfast served. Daddy comes in from the outside, morning newspaper in hand. He stands in front of his chair, drops his pajamas and sits in the chair before realizing he's not in the bathroom. He was so focused on reading the headlines; he succumbed to his normal morning ritual, reading the paper while on his throne Red faced, he yanked up those PJs in record time. We all busted a gut.

Not long before the tomato blooper, he arrived at his dental appointment without one important item. He had left his teeth at home. No, daddy doing odd things was not uncommon. Even so, there was something different lately; something tough to pinpoint. Laughing it off wasn't quite getting it, but he was Daddy, after all.

T. Allen Winn

Mama witnessed more and more strange events by him. Some she shared with us, most she didn't. She refused to admit that Daddy had some serious issues, but in the meantime her patience grew thin. She began taking it out on him. No one seemed to give it much thought, what he might be wrestling with, his life apparently busting loose at the seams.

Daddy's golfing buddies noticed his game had begun deteriorating, not that he ever was a master of the fairways. Shooting in triple digits, he didn't have much of a golf game to start with. Ignoring the signs seems so much easier. His cronies didn't see the significance. Like us, they had witnessed the lighter side.

A defining moment, the battle of the hot water heater would open a crack in the door; to give us a glimpse of *Houston we do have a serious problem*. Mama noticed that the water temperature had diminished when washing dishes or running bath water. She suspected a faulty thermostat in the hot water heater or maybe it was just time to replace it all together. She called a plumber to come check it out.

The plumber reported that all checked fine. He had discovered that the temperature setting had been set too low, so he adjusted it. All returned to normal temporarily. A few days later Mama realized the tap water in the kitchen was luke-warm again. She asked Daddy to check it and he said it was fine, adding that someone was going to get badly scalded by it.

The Care Giver's Son

She asked him if he had turned down the thermostat setting. He confessed he had, but only to prevent anyone from being injured. Of course she went off on him and then had a brother-in-law reset it when Daddy refused. It never dawned on any of us that Daddy was struggling with how to control the tap water from the faucet. He had evidently only switched the water to hot, no blend, and his solution, reduce the temperature in the water heater. Perhaps he had already had close calls without us knowing it.

A day or so later the thermostat had again been adjusted by him. Mama freaked and raked him over the coals. By now she knew how to reset it and did. They volleyed back and forth several times, with her blessing him out each time he countered. Finally it just came to an abrupt end. He became disinterested and just stopped fiddling with it, just like that. It sure saved him additional butt chewing from the resident-ranter.

I didn't condone what he had been doing but tended to take sides with him because I resented how she argued with and belittled him in front of others. Guess I inherited that from her because I never took Mama's crap. She and I could go at it nose to nose, neither giving an inch. Daddy always did. He never put up a good fight; just allowed her to get it out of her system. I had never heard him raise his voice to her. That was about to change too. The caregiver was going to be tested very soon.

Not to forget about Mama's other responsibility; Granny had her good days and bad days. The bad days were winning most of the time but she remained strong and determined to stay at her house. That would be changing very soon also.

Fast forwarding, my year living with my folks had finally come to an end. I had a new wife, new house and new job, and thus far had not been sucked into the ever expanding whirlpool. Mama took care of things, as always.

The only care that interested me was that of which I gave to my wife and our new life. Well, let me clarify that. You could always count on me, if you asked for my help. I'd be there, sometimes kicking and screaming, but would be there all the same. I lacked the motivation to act or react on my own. Don't ask me. I have no clue what makes me be like this. I'm a defective human I suppose.

Ignoring their needs was no longer an option. My new wife made sure I did the right thing even if it wasn't my idea. She served as my alter ego. She was good at it and I certainly required the push. I did it without as much of a fight. Could I be learning? Me, probably not...

Even though I suspect she knew better, Mama kept pushing Daddy along to do the things they enjoyed doing, except I'm not sure

The Care Giver's Son

Daddy expressed the same jubilation. He seemed to be withdrawing into some sort of shell. The undertow had us in its grip, but I didn't feel the riptide yet. I can tread water.

Granny's physical condition continued to deteriorate. Mentally she was still sharp as ever but physically she couldn't do a lot of the things she had always done. She finally gave up having her little vegetable garden and could only do light house work. Mama had Daddy do Granny's vacuuming, but even this challenged him. The bells were going off.

Granny still cooked and managed to make it to the grocery store and to church, but that was about the extent of her activities. Super caregiver stepped in and did the rest. I kept the bench warm, except for when my wife booted me into the lineup. She wore those boots quite well. I can't say I didn't deserve it.

Daddy continued to misplace items; his wallet, his watch, his ring, his belt and his teeth. He tried to cover up and hide these little situations but, oh no, Mama wouldn't allow it. She rubbed his nose in them, determined to point out how he should know better. That's what she did and she was stubborn as a dog with a bone. My wife and I were a little more understanding and tried to give him free passes, even though we weren't sure what was going on at the time.

He'd started doing things like leaving car doors open or the car running when he did a grocery run. To conceal his forgetfulness, he began asking my wife's assistance when he tried to dress himself, shirts, socks, belt. She kept this their little secret and didn't let on to Mama that he was struggling with everyday details. She would not have been so forgiving.

Mama eventually took over the yard care duties when Daddy didn't stay on top of his chores. Oh, she gave him an ear full each and every time. Sadly, she drove that riding lawnmower with reckless abandon. You'd see sparks flying as she mowed close to the side walk out front, with the mower blade much too low. The caregiver wasn't necessarily the best choice for doing lawn care. Caregiver didn't equate to caretaker. You couldn't tell her that.

It was now too obvious to ignore, even for me. Daddy had some serious issues and it wasn't getting any better. The caregiver had little patience in the matter. I had a hard time dealing with their bickering. Well, maybe bickering is the wrong term. Mama did the raising cane, fussing and correcting poor old Daddy. Daddy didn't argue back. I just wished once; he would stand his ground.

I tried to convince Mama to let it be when he made a mistake, but then she and I would go a round or two. We were both good at doing this. She would not concede and give him a pass, and I wouldn't give her one. She'd throw up every episode in his face. It became almost

The Care Giver's Son

unbearable for me. I was becoming quite resentful of her treatment of him.

My dear wife had her hands full, keeping me calmed down and off Mama's back. The caregiver wasn't always so caring when it came to her own husband. And me, I wasn't caring at all. Of course I only witnessed snippets, but oh how I hated those snippets.

As mentioned several times previously, Mama and Daddy loved to go on cruises, so we decided we would go with them on another one. We would help her cattle prod Daddy along. Two other couples joined us. How did that go, you ask? Not so good! Just getting Daddy from one end of the ship to the other turned out to be a major task.

The first part of our trip included a couple of days in Orlando so we decided to visit the theme parks, Disney and Universal. The Magic Kingdom turned out to be not so magical. With much opposition and reluctance, we convinced Daddy to allow us to push him around the Magic Kingdom in a wheelchair. This became a very humbling experience for him and the rest of us.

It did have its perks though. By his being in the wheelchair, we moved to the front of the line for all rides. I saw him laugh for the first time in many months when we rode the Universal Studio's Jaws boat adventure. Every time the shark attacked the boat his laughter became contagious for us all. I still have some great candid photos of him and the shark. I am especially glad we brought him along. The next part of the vacation, the cruise, would be a journey into Adventure Land.

The man that had once only possessed one speed, wide open now had only first gear. Oh how this was totally unacceptable to Mama. This introduced many challenges on board the ship. Fortunately, six other caregivers rallied to the cause and relieved Mama of most of her duties so she could have some downtime and enjoy HER cruise.

Daddy could no longer be trusted to go to the public restrooms by himself, so I accompanied him while on the ship. The restrooms onboard had two doors, one as an entrance way and the second opening to the bathroom. When we passed through the first door, I had to restrain Daddy from unzipping his pants immediately. I had begun my caregiver training; I just didn't comprehend it.

We had early seating for dinner and the eight of us had our own table. My wife or her sister always positioned themselves between Daddy and Mama so they could carve up his food. They made sure they watched over his eating habits. They encouraged the caregiver to have another adult beverage or three to just keep her on a tranquilized pace. Servers noticed his woes and began pre-carving his food. The staff was wonderful with him.

The Care Giver's Son

Somehow we survived the voyage but realized we had probably taken Daddy on his last cruise. We weren't sure what the future held for Mama, being the perfect picture of health, and trapped in this new prison with Daddy.

Granny's physical health continued to decline, but she did not give up her little house. Mama continued to maintain two households, hers and Granny's. She still pushed Daddy along, continuing the Saturday night dances, their escape; or I should say it was hers.

Mama enjoyed these little romps. I'm not sure that Daddy did. His conversational skills had dwindled considerably and he seldom danced now. The women folk were persistent and would get him on the dance floor a couple of times. We kept the caregiver occupied so Daddy would not have to be exposed to the fussing from her. In that sense, the outings were probably good for him too.

I still tried to keep my distance from the unfolding saga, except on Sundays when we always ate dinner and supper with them. Does this sound familiar? We did this at Granny's while Papa faltered. A family draws on family in good times and bad.

I guess the window cracked open just a tad for me. I saw that I was losing my Dad. I still didn't have much sympathy for Mama, still resenting her continued verbal assaults on Daddy. Caregiver or not, the behavior was totally unacceptable to me. Leave the man alone, I would tell her. My rants fell on deaf ears, the pigheaded pair we were.

Mama continued to push him. We, along with Mama, Daddy, and another couple took a vacation to New Orleans, driving my folk's leisure van. Daddy now required assistance in dressing, bathing, bathroom and eating. This depressed even me.

The goal for the rest of us continued to be that of temporary caregivers. This ensured both Mama and Daddy received a break from the action and each other, Mama being the primary caregiver, and Daddy not having to receive her wrath for doing things wrong or too slowly.

We brought a wheelchair on this trip to help us get Daddy from one place to the next. He no longer opposed it but who could say if he really accepted it. He rarely said anything now.

We did make one grave error on one of our excursions. The shuttle would pick us up at the hotel and make all of our connections throughout the day. Research indicated that we would have use of a wheelchair when we toured the New Orleans Aquarium and again when we did a dinner cruise down the Mississippi. The old river paddle boat would eventually take us to the zoo. The zoo had wheel chairs. We took turns pushing him, excluding Mama from her turn.

The return cruise on the old river boat included meals and entertainment. We overlooked one detail of our little outing. Arriving back at the dock we discovered that the return shuttle would be located many blocks away. We could follow the river walk but no longer had the luxury of a wheelchair. This would test Daddy and the rest of us.

Our little nighttime trek first began with us traveling at Daddy's pace. The clock didn't allow for this because we were faced with missing the shuttle. We encouraged him to pick up the pace and tried to make a game out of it. This only worked in spurts. The frustrations ran high as we were faced with the fact we'd not make our shuttle connection. Daddy labored to make the jaunt.

When we finally reached our destination, we were faced with our next challenge. We had indeed missed the first shuttle. The next one would be by in an hour. Our long river walk had obviously taken a toll on Daddy both physically and mentally. With nowhere to sit down, we had to prop him up and constantly talk to him, reassuring him this ordeal would soon be over. Mama, now livid, had required therapy too. The caregiver had reached the end of her rope.

For the first time I really thought Daddy may not make it the next hour. His heavy breathing and pale complexion strained on his facial expressions. The five of us had obviously flunked Caregiver's 101. I took a pass because

I'd not taken the course. It was back to the bench for me, a place best suited for me.

This would be Daddy's last vacation trip and possibly Mama's too. Life of the caregiver is so unjust. I was glad I wasn't one. I closed the window once again. That's what I do best.

Mama assumed her role as the primary caregiver once again and I let her. That's what she does best. Daddy had no say in the matter, trapped in a life he had not chosen and a body that he no longer controlled. Hell would soon have a new name, Alzheimer's.

> One person caring about another represents life's greatest value
> **Jim Rohn**

The Care Giver's Son

Queen Solomon's Dilemma

What is a caregiver to do? Whether Mama wished to admit it or not, Daddy had a serious health issue that needed to be addressed and identified. All of her yelling at him couldn't magically bring about a cure. She finally conceded and we took him to the doctor. The doctor recommended a specialist. And the verdict is...

To everyone's surprise the specialist diagnosed him with a type of Parkinson disease. This wasn't the shaky kind, but instead caused Daddy's muscles to become rigid. The term, Parkinsonism became part of our ever growing terminology. The medical term, Alzheimer's was tossed out there too, but the doctor said it could not be diagnosed as easily. He suspected Daddy's affliction to be a cross between the two. Just lovely, he had a two-for; a man that had never been sick in his life until that silent heart attack.

Now you would think the news would impact Mama and how she dealt with the situation, but it really didn't. She still corrected him when he did or said something wrong. She had very little tolerance. We tried to convince her to go along with him but she wouldn't. She flatly refused to allow him to be wrong or sick. I showed up on Sundays and anguished over her chastising of Daddy.

T. Allen Winn

Mama came to a crossroad. She could no longer maintain two households, hers and Granny's. She served Granny an ultimatum. She would have to move in with my folks. She did. Mama hired someone to maintain her yard and continued to assist, while Granny paid the utilities to a house she was no longer using. She was such a good caregiver. I was behind her 100%; way behind her, except on Sundays, and then I would do what I needed to do.

Granny had her own bedroom and bathroom in the three bedroom ranch style home. Mama gave up tending to their yard and hired someone to do it for her, the same service she used for Granny's. A friend would sit in when she had to run to the grocery or to her weekly hairdresser appointment. Their lives came to a screeching halt otherwise.

With Granny now living under roof, the Saturday night dancing at the Anderson VFW became a thing of the past, caregiver's curse. This might have been a blessing in disguise for Daddy, as he wasn't up to it, even though Mama really needed the outlet.

Over the next year she continued managing Granny's bills, utilities and yard maintenance from Granny's monthly check. She finally informed Granny she needed to sell her little mill house. Obviously Granny would never be able to return to it, and it had become a financial liability and too time consuming for Mama. I worried how Granny would take this.

The Care Giver's Son

The pain on Granny's face told the story. She really didn't want to part with her home, but she did as Mama had asked, realizing the burden on her shoulders. Her house and most of her belonging were auctioned off. We salvaged anything she wanted to keep and kept other things for ourselves. Her old Chevy Impala ended up selling for the same price she had paid for it when it came off the train thirty years prior, $2200.

The caregiver had all her patients under one roof and no more liabilities to deal with, so life pushed onward. I'm glad she could do this; actually wanted to do this. I certainly had no desire to follow in her footsteps. I'd continue to be there on Sundays though, a cameo is better than nothing I suppose.

My Mama transformed into Granny, possessed I think, or maybe Granny was just rubbing off on her. She expected us to be there all the time. She didn't like it when we traveled. She could put the guilt trip on us in a heartbeat. Granny should have been proud of her prodigy, two peas in a pod they were.

Mama became buried in self pity, another part of the caregiver's curse. That would be her curse, not mine. She would have to live with the choices she made. Not me, I still had a life. I wasn't cut out to walk in her shoes. We still helped her, but I did it when it was convenient for me, or on Sundays, or when my wife told me to. I did what I must.

T. Allen Winn

In the meantime we had moved into our newly built house about twenty minutes away. We brought the clan over when we were just moving in. Because the windows had been up and doors open, the house had become infested with flies. We each manned a fly swatter and marched into battle. We even gave Daddy a swatter.

After hours of swatting these pesky winged critters, it appeared we had finally won the battle. I confiscated the weapons and let everyone have a well deserved break. Daddy continued to swat at the air with an imaginary fly swatter. At times like these you had to laugh about it. The caregiver even laughed and didn't try to correct him. Now that had to be a defining moment even if it had been short lived.

Daddy had to use the facilities. Mama was busy at the time. Bathroom duty defaulted to me. I accompanied him to the restroom. I positioned Daddy in front of the toilet and waited. He just stood there. I unzipped his pants and told him to pee. He just stood there. I squatted beside him, and then removed his manhood from his pants. I held it, taking careful aim. He began to pee.

Before he completed his task, he looked down at me and said, "You know, it's pretty sad when your son has to hold your pecker while you pee." I am usually quick with comebacks, but I didn't have one this time. I

The Care Giver's Son

zipped him up, assisted him with washing his hands. I'm not sure why I did that because he hadn't touched anything. I then lead him back to the couch where he began swatting those pesky imaginary flies again with his likewise imaginary swatter. I guess I earned my honorary caregiver wings that day but didn't want to admit it.

A lot of my story includes tales of those inflicted with diseases beyond our control, but you couldn't have a caregiver without those that require the care. It seems like we had no shortage of the latter. We were skimpy on the caregivers but Mama could carry the load. That was her gift.

We brought Daddy, Mama and Granny over to our new house regularly to show them new items and the progress we were making. The yard had no shortage of rocks and while walking Daddy around the perimeter, he would scoop them up and toss them, thinking he was tossing them out of the way. I never let on.

He was really just depositing them to another part of the yard. I just laughed it off and allowed him to do his thing. Mama would have corrected him if she'd seen him do it. We kept this our little father-son secret or at least I did. Daddy was oblivious to the fact.

On another occasion, the clan sat on the front porch while I finished mowing the yard and weed-eating the drive. I fired up the gas blower and gave it to Daddy. He traveled the full length blowing the debris off our driveway, which extended several hundred feet. I think he enjoyed doing it, but one can never know.

We laughed as we watched him work his magic. I think it probably restored some of his self esteem. It wasn't the perfect blow job, but who cared. Even Mama didn't intervene this time. That surprised everyone. Maybe there was hope for her after all. That's more than I could say for me. We'd both have to work on our little problems.

Daddy, stricken with this dreadful Parkinson and Alzheimer's much too young, he had long ago quit his weekly golfing. He no longer possessed the motor skills or mental capacity to play the game he had loved. He and I took up the game at different times in life. We had conflicting schedules and had very few opportunities to play a round together. I can probably count on one hand how many times we actually did.

He never played the game during my years as a young man still living in the household, nor did I. I flew the nest at eighteen and didn't play my first round until the ripe old age of twenty. I sucked at it and never took the game seriously.

Over the years I played the game in spurts, often playing no more than three or four times a year. I don't think I began playing with any regularity until about the age of forty five, playing our Wednesday Whomper afternoons

The Care Giver's Son

with coworkers. I still sucked but so did my playing partners. We enjoyed the fellowship.

Daddy didn't take up the game until after his early retirement from the textile mill. In his late fifties he had decided to begin playing with three of his cronies a couple of times a week at a nine-hole course, High Meadows Country Club, same place I whacked my first ball. I think one of his buddies gave him a used bag and set of clubs. It looked like a starter set.

I worked days back then and they played mornings so tee times seldom worked out for us. The first time I did play with him I realized, father like son, he sucked too. I guess I inherited my hacking ways. I now know why the father-son team never played the game routinely. We could stink up a round.

Earlier, with Daddy still in perfect health and playing a round with his nephew and friends, he decided to hit his next shot. The foursome putting out on the green ahead were in no danger of his short distance worm burners, a shot I also have mastered. You guessed it. He nailed one, hitting one of the unsuspecting four golfers in the leg.

Daddy, not necessarily known for his strategy on the links, quickly handed his club to his nephew, Bob, and then he walked toward the cart. He was left holding the bag or club in this case. Bob waved and begged forgiveness and, luckily for them, the foursome accepted the unfortunate great shot as accidental. I think they even left the ball on the green. I never did ask what Daddy shot on that hole, not that it matters now.

When his health declined, as mentioned earlier, he eventually walked away from the game. A young man in his sixties, that silent heart attack followed by the Parkinson and the twist of Alzheimer's had sealed his fate. Cruel diseases they are. One punishes the body while the other steals the mind.

His illnesses had reduced him to a mere shell of a man. We did the best to keep him involved. We brought Mama, Granny and him over to our house one Sunday for a little family gathering and cook out. The guys consisting of bothers-in-law and nephews decided to play Par 3 West, a local nine-hole par three course just up the street, all five playing from my bag. I brought Daddy along, thinking it would be good for him.

He still had some motor skills but rarely articulated more than a one or two word sentence at best. His face had lost all expression, and I'd catch myself wondering what he might be thinking, or if he was even capable of provocative thought. One will never know I suppose.

On the first tee box, I regretted my decision. I teed up his ball for him, gave him a nine iron but sadly, he couldn't comprehend what direction to hit the ball. My heart ached when he addressed the ball in the opposite direction

The Care Giver's Son

of the green, no more than one hundred ten yards behind him.

Each hole thereafter, I aligned and positioned him for every shot. His shuffle walk became increasingly challenged by the contour of the course. Another bad on my part, I hadn't considered his inability to walk the course. There were no riding carts.

I agonized, watching him hole after hole knowing he shouldn't been there, but we tried to push on and complete the nine hole round. He did make contact most of the time, once I positioned him in front of the tee and got quickly out of his way. Robotic is the best I can explain it, each swing appeared so mechanical and rigid.

Number six, one hundred thirty yards, clutching his shoulders, I strategically positioned and aimed him for the green. His shot worm-burned thirty yards off the tee. I guided him to his ball and realigned him for the next shot. He struck that same nine iron, holing the rounds only bird from a hundred yards.

The five of us started whooping and hollering, not believing what we had just witnessed. We began patting him on the back and telling him what he had done. The joy on his face was priceless. He actually laughed, and I really believe he understood the feat he had just pulled off.

Regrets extinguished. We could have quit then, because I had just experienced my best round of golf. For me, he joined the immortals that day at Number Six.

Now I've really gotten the mileage from that story. I never grow tired of telling it to anyone who will listen. I even submitted it to a writing contest once on The Golf Channel. I'm glad Mama didn't accompany us that afternoon, because she would have badgered him the entire round and probably would not have experienced the magic.

Daddy would never pick up another golf club. There would be no mulligan. He finished on top though. I'll always remember the miracle shot, his final birdie.

Daddy entered a new phase. He began having these walking spurts. He couldn't stop walking and would walk through the house until the perspiration literally poured off him or until he fell. This had something to do with the Parkinsonism. His limbs would stiffen up and he would lose his balance.

Sometimes he could get up on his own. Other times, Mama would have to recruit help to get him on his feet or to his recliner. I came, if asked, and when I wasn't at work. Most of the time my uncle or a friend was close by so my services weren't required. I returned to my spot on the bench, my rightful place.

Daddy also began to have these little violent episodes where he'd no longer take Mama's crap. I thought I would be happy to finally see him take up for himself. I wasn't. He began

The Care Giver's Son

cursing like nobody I had ever heard. Sound familiar; Papa did this too, neither possessing the typical salty language. Mama just entered mortal combat, refusing to give in no matter how many times we asked her to just let it go. That really angered me, her doing this to him.

One particular morning while Mama assisted him in the bathroom, he grabbed her by the arms and pushed her into the corner and against the bathroom window. She fought him as if she were being attacked by a rapist. She told us that she didn't care about his mental problems. She said no man was going to manhandle her like that. She'd kill him first. Things you don't want to hear come from your Mama's mouth. We had reached a new turning point. The curse of the caregiver had raised its ugly head once again.

Caregiving is really such a thankless job, so I've heard. I wouldn't know because I had not yet walked a mile in those shoes, not full time. Being a relief pitcher in the late innings I had only experienced it in brief cameo appearances. My save percentage would not make the record books, a record I would never be proud of possessing. But then again, being in the game did not rank high on my priority list. I don't know what makes me think this way. It defies explanation, even for me.

Mama had the million dollar arm and enjoyed the limelight. I stood back and allowed her to bask in it for better or worse, and toss those fast balls. I could do that because I am good at it. Warning, don't try this at home. Leave it to the professionals! I'm not one.

Now sarcasm is something I'm good at. It serves as a mask possibly, to hide my real feelings, that and my quick wit. These are tools of my trade. I get caught up in me too easily. It's a tricky defense system at best and can often backfire. I'm not sure if I'm fearful of the caregiving or just not willing to watch those that I love implode. I don't think I'm a bad person, but then again, maybe I am. One thing for sure, those that I love continued to be stricken with sickness, illnesses I never knew existed. I handled it poorly.

Daddy attempted to conceal his mistakes. He'd hide soiled underwear or other clothing. This new hide and seek competition kept Mama on top of her game, bringing out a much worse bad side, worse than any of us could ever imagine.

Daddy continued to lure my wife into the game when he became challenged putting on a shirt or buttoning the shirt. Socks, belts and shoes offered similar struggles. He covertly recruited her to follow him to the bedroom or hallway without tipping off Mama.

She always assisted him, never letting on to Mama of his struggles. Mama would only go off on him and he didn't deserve that. She didn't cope well with his inability to do just

The Care Giver's Son

simple tasks as dress himself, and this tested my patience with her, out constant battle.

Even a healthy Daddy had always allowed Mama to run roughshod over him. I faulted him for that because I had always stood my ground with her. I now faulted Mama for stripping him of his dignity when she could as easily let it go and not rub his nose in it.

It sounds like I'm picking sides, doesn't it? I felt he needed the support more than she did. He did, but I didn't see the whole picture from my viewpoint outside the window. Mama's life suffered dramatically, but I only felt Daddy's pain.

Thankfully, Granny could take care of herself. She moved slowly and had her own bag of physical restrictions, but she didn't require any constant care or major assistance to perform her daily activities. That would change in due time. The caregiver continued to focus on her primary patient, but her bitterness grew like a tick gorging itself in a blood bank.

Her life had been stolen in a time when she should have been enjoying retirement. Daddy would say the same thing, if capable of articulating it. They both had been dealt such a lousy hand. We never know what destiny has in store for us. We work all our lives, hopeful of a fulfilled retirement. Life isn't always fair.

Daddy began falling...a lot. Those walking spells and falling spells were taking their toll on him as well as Mama. He would make circles through the house until he lost his balance and fell. Parkinsonism slammed him with a vengeance. During this turbulent time he had been extremely lucky that he never hurt himself severely during these freefalls.

If nobody was around to help her get him up, Mama would assist him when he fell by positioning him close to a piece of furniture. She would then help him pull up and get to his feet. Sometimes it worked, more often it didn't. When it didn't she'd call a family member or friend to come over and help. Daddy would remain on the floor until the Calvary arrived. I often wondered what he was thinking during those times he sat on the floor.

Granny experienced bouts of congestive heart failure, sending her to the emergency room via the ambulance and leading to an eventual hospital stay each time. We'd alternate caregiver duties. My wife and I would go to the hospital, and then swap out with Mama, staying with Daddy while she visited the hospital.

Those emergency phone calls usually came in the middle of night. Wish Granny could have planned better. This really played havoc on my personal life. My wife kept me in check and focused on my responsibilities. She was much more responsible than I; thank goodness for that and for her.

Daddy's health deteriorated to the point that he could not walk on his own. His home healthcare nurse convinced Mama to use a

The Care Giver's Son

wheelchair and hospital bed for him. We ended up dismantling my parent's bedroom to make it spacious and friendly with a hospital bed for Daddy and single bed for Mama. The nurse, a very close family friend had become instrumental in Daddy's and Granny's home health care. She was an angel sent to us.

The new routine consisted of pulling and tugging Daddy from bed, standing him up, slipping him into the wheel chair, and then making our way to his recliner. There we reversed the routine settling him in his chair. Daddy didn't complain. I'm not sure he could.

He really had no choice in the matter. A blessing in disguise, his inability to walk made it easier on Mama because now she could better control the situation. For her it had always been all about control. Daddy falling was no longer a fear.

Easier came with a price. Manhandling him to get him from one place to the other wore on Mama's weary bones. My wife and I got a taste of it on Sundays during our weekly visit. Things got worse. He could no longer feed himself. The bar just got raised a little higher for Mama, the ultimate caregiver and warrior.

Granny continued to take care of her own needs and could still feed herself. The scales were beginning to tip in Father Times' favor though, the clock ticked faster. Granny's day was growing near.

T. Allen Winn

We tend to take the little things for granted. I'm no different in that perspective. I was slowly but surely getting it, I suppose. Witnessing Daddy slip away was tough. I didn't at this time consider what effect his disease was having on Mama. After all, she was a rock and the perfect picture of health.

Granny had been sick all of her life. This allowed her to fly under the radar screen most of the time. We reacted when she had one of her spells. I can't tell you how many times we thought we had lost her. I think she hung on because she thought Mama needed her.

I guess if we live long enough we tend to backslide toward our childhood. Memory goes. We often find ourselves toothless again and our motor skills limited. We lose body mass and shrink, I'm told. You don't think this way until finally you realize you're on the backside of your life. You can only hope for a long healthy life.

Daddy now wore Depends. I used to laugh about those adult diaper commercials. Now they didn't seem nearly so funny. A wife shouldn't have to change her husband's diaper. I didn't have children of my own so I had never changed one in my life. You certainly don't need your first time to be your Daddy's.

I sure dwell on how these changes impacted my life, never giving it a thought about how it had impacted his. Even further from my thought pattern, how it had impacted Mama's. I

The Care Giver's Son

was getting it in some sense but still had a long way to go to fully understand the magnitude. My day would surely come. Today just wasn't that day.

T. Allen Winn

The Double Sided Sword

Life's journey can take each of us down unique paths. While I believe somewhat in destiny, I still think we can influence the quality of the ride by the choices we make along the way. So far I had not chosen wisely when it came to family health issues. I still had a glimmer of hope because many more miles remained before reaching the final destination. Could there really be hope, even for me?

I fully understood the ramifications of Daddy's downward spiral. I realized medically that it could not be altered. He had become a one hundred fifty pound infant. He could no longer do anything for himself. Home Healthcare now visited several times weekly to take care of his hygienic needs. Mama filled in between visits. Our nurse friend checked on him several times a week; regretfully, more than I did. As a son, I should have known the pecking order.

Granny tried to help Mama as much as she could, but her physical capabilities were limited and diminishing quickly. Still, just being there helped Mama tremendously. Mama could at least run errands knowing she no longer had to worry about Daddy getting into any mischief. Both Daddy and Granny now owned lift recliners. This did nothing for the décor of the den, the new assisted living facility.

The Care Giver's Son

Granny had another one of those *almost heart congestive failure attacks*, requiring an ambulance transport. This time we thought certainly she would not return from the hospital. She somehow survived and returned back home, this time actually saying Mama needed her help. Now more than ever, I think that's what kept her alive and kicking. Life throws its curves, but somehow things work out.

Unfortunately, she now required more of Mama's care than she could offer in return. Mama had two to care for and would be challenged to kick it up a notch. She could handle it. That's what she does. We'd see her on Sunday and do our part.

My wife and I still worked full time and lived in an adjacent town. We would be there, if they needed us, but we couldn't be there all the time. Living in a small town, Mama always had other friends and family dropping by to check on them. They'd relieve Mama long enough for her to do her grocery runs, her hair appointments and other various errands.

Unable to transport Daddy's limp body from bed to chair and back using the wheelchair, a hydraulic lift became the mechanism that made this journey still possible. Mama, determined to place him in the chair, would make the move daily. We did it for her on Sundays, or any other days we happened to be there.

T. Allen Winn

By now we had purchased and read a book about the symptoms of Alzheimer's. Mama and my wife had even attended a workshop to better understand this wicked disease. Two of my Dad's brothers had started showing the signs of this devastating dignity taker.

One had been diagnosed with an advanced case. While neither of his brothers had become bedridden, we could certainly see the textbook signs sneaking up on them. The one uncle refused to read the book and suffered from denial. Me, I just wondered if this would be my eventual fate too. Now wouldn't that just serve me right?

Migrating from her bed to her chair each day became Granny's event. Her mind still sharp as a tack, but the old body just couldn't keep up with her wants. Mama had to pick up the slack like she always did. She was tough and stubborn. I inherited these traits honestly.

Somewhere in the birth canal I had lost some of her positive attributes though. Not that I didn't care, but mine didn't come so open ended as did hers. I would still have my opportunities if I so chose to act on them. Why didn't I choose the right path? That remained the question.

You have a tendency to look for the little things in situations like this to brighten up your day and improve your outlook on life. For us, anytime we could get a smile or better still, a laugh from Daddy, it was a good day. It almost

The Care Giver's Son

feels like it does when you try to get an infant to react to your foolishness.

Daddy rarely ever spoke a word now days, so we didn't know what he needed or might be thinking. He ate what his feeder fed him and couldn't complain if he didn't like it. Was he full or hungry was anyone's guess. On Sundays my wife or I were the designated feeders, to give Mama a break. More often my wife performed this task. I let her, but would do it, if I had to; what a son.

Some Sundays I pulled baby sitter duty, allowing my wife to take Mama shopping and leave the caregiving behind for the afternoon. I had no problem stepping up to the plate when asked, and I did just fine in this role. Pity, I had to be asked to take care of my Granny and Daddy, don't you think? Family and friends typically revolved through the doorway, so Sundays were rarely what I'd call "kick-back afternoons." I sure liked kicking back.

Over the next stretch it seems having an ambulance parked in front of my parent's house had become a frequent event. This kept the neighbors guessing. Who would they be transporting to hospital this time, Daddy or Granny? Each time either of them was admitted to the hospital, we felt it would be their last. They always seemed to spring back better than new. The caregiver waited in the wings for their return. I just waited, not yet embracing my role. How pathetic is that?

Mama would never admit it but this caregiver stuff had been slowly taking a toll on her. The constant lifting and straining to move Daddy, and staying a step ahead of Granny had wreaked havoc on her back. We had tried to convince her to hire some part time help, but it always fell on deaf ears. She too much enjoyed her role as the martyr, and she didn't hesitate to play that card to her advantage.

No one can dispute the fact that she had lost control of her life in her prime, at a time when she and Daddy should be enjoying the fruits of their labor. But remember, she chose to be the caregiver. She refused to allow either Granny or Daddy to receive professional care outside the home. Choices come with consequences.

Everything had to be on her terms and at her house. She would not compromise her beliefs. Arguing with her was pointless. You can't wallow in the mud with a pig and expect to win. She could wallow with the best of them.

The Caregiver's Caregiver

You know how the saying goes; you can't help those who are not willing to help themselves. This is easy to say coming from one hard head talking about another, cursed with the same trait. The martyr syndrome prevailed and had actually run its course with us.

I remembered the line from the movie, *Network*, 'I'm mad as hell and won't take this any more!' I almost screamed it from an open window like in the movie. It would have probably felt good to do so. I'm sure others would have benefited from similar behavior.

Mama had learned from the best, her mother. Granny, an expert at laying the guilt trip on you, had trained the little grasshopper. Mama could snatch the pebble from her hand effortlessly. Sorry, I succumbed to a Kungfu moment; however, the analogy did fit.

I guess living under the same roof had rubbed off on Mama. Their mannerisms were so similar now that it had almost become difficult to tell them apart. I didn't like, nor appreciate, this transformation. I had conceded to losing Daddy. Where had Mama gone? She looked like my Mama, but she certainly no longer acted like my Mama.

Mama, the once throw caution to the wind, live on the edge and enjoy life to the fullest, vibrant female had become an old and bitter woman suddenly. She now worried about everything we did. Truth be known, if her situation had not impacted her ability to go, she would have still been right there with us.

She encouraged us to enjoy life while we could, but that was just the set-up statement. Master martyr, she followed that up with a zinger in an attempt to guilt us out of our decision to do whatever we wanted to do and replaced it with what she wanted us to do. She was good at making us feel guilty. She really needed the escape and would have loved being with us, no matter where it took her.

This had to stop for her sake and our sanity. *The Martyr Syndrome, the Ultimate Guide for Manipulation and Guilt Transformation* has a catchy title for a book. She could be my co-author or paid consultant. Her picture would definitely be on the front cover.

We made one more pitch for her to seek a helper, someone that could relieve her of her caregiver responsibilities so she could have more freedom. She would not relinquish this so easily because doing so would compromise her being the martyr. I think she truly enjoyed this role.

How could she draw pity from others if she was out enjoying life while those requiring her care remained at home? What would others think of her? She enjoyed this role way too much to allow someone else to steal her thunder. She was good at it and we were sick of

The Care Giver's Son

it. To our shock she agreed to consider finding a helper.

My wife and I pitied the person that would have to undergo her scrutiny. After all, as we had already discovered, no one did it like she did it. She frequently pointed this out to us when we tried to help. Where would we find this perfect person? We needed to act quickly before she changed her mind, so our search began.

Our dilemma, recruit someone that would meet Mama's expectations and would be compatible with Granny. Where would we find this Mama clone? Greater powers were at work here. Like manna from heaven, a name surfaced; someone I knew well, a person from my childhood.

We had struck gold or so it seemed. The Clone already performed caregiver duties at another household, so she certainly had the required experience. Her being a member of Granny's church shifted the tide in our favor. Mama knew her too and she lived no more than ten minutes away. It seemed too good to be true, like low hanging fruit. The question remained, would she pass the Mama test?

We contacted her and she came over for a visit to see just exactly what we had in mind. I had not seen her in too many years to count. She assessed the situation and committed to giving it a try a couple of days a week. She would split duty between Daddy and her other patient.

Mama walked her through her routine to ensure the potential Clone followed her letter of the law. We held our breath and tried not to get our hopes up. Both Mama and Granny could make this null and void on a whim. The test drive completed, everyone seemed happy with the arrangement. It was time to celebrate.

Mama eventually took advantage of the Clone's days on duty and actually got out of the house for a change. My wife made a point of taking her shopping or out for dinner engagements with friends. Mama had all the appearances of a liberated woman.

Granny even enjoyed the new caregiver's company. As for Daddy, we couldn't be sure, but it probably did him good to not have Mama around. She could still be a little abrasive with him at times. Things were looking up. I liked it. Selfishly, I was sort of off the hook. One has to be on the hook before one can be off the hook.

Life for Mama had turned a corner. She was back to enjoying it a little. Her protégée had transformed into more of a Mama Clone than we could have ever visualized. She did light cleaning, the laundry and tended to Daddy and Granny to a standard that met Mama's complete approval. That's something that I had never been able to achieve, even before this caregiving stuff.

The Care Giver's Son

Mama enjoyed her new found freedom so much that she increased the number of days that her replacement worked weekly and even used her for partial days on the weekend. We hated to tell her we told her so, but we had encouraged her to find this sort of help years ago. Oh well, it was working and that was all that counted. We were still expected there on Sundays, though.

After she reached her comfort zone with the new caregiver, we enticed her into taking a weekend off. Reluctant at first because she worried how the world would scrutinize her, leaving Granny and Daddy for a weekend, she finally agreed to go off with us to our beach condo for a relaxing weekend.

Still concerned that she would lose that martyr status, she milked the moment with family and friends. She assured them that my wife and I had coerced her into this little trip. Fine, we'd take the blame. Everyone but Mama knew she needed it. Neither her family nor friends would pull the type of guilt trip on her that she normally pulled on us. Strangely, we faced a Sunday in our future that we'd not spend at Mama's house.

The beach trip turned out to be beneficial for all. Mama actually enjoyed herself after getting beyond the "they can't do without me" stage. It did Granny and Daddy good for Mama to not be there for a change. We all survived and did some serious soul searching. Our weekend stay turned out to be uneventful on the larger scale. No ambulances or morticians were required at the beach or at home. The world spun without Mama there to take care of matters.

While being ravished by these two dreaded diseases and living life as an invalid, Daddy had lost a brother to Alzheimer's, a second brother to unfortunate health problems and a sister to cancer. We're not even sure if he comprehended these losses because he displayed no emotion when told.

Two of his golfing buddies had also passed. It's funny how life works out. He just kept ticking along, vital signs good and health not so bad either, considering his condition. Friends and family were dropping like flies. Life can be so ironic.

Our Home Healthcare friend kept him in check. She saw to Granny's needs. Both were on a catheter now so that required close watching. Mama enjoyed her every visit like some social event. We continued our Sunday routine. Mama became less of martyr or maybe we just didn't pay it as much attention.

We seemed to have crept over the mountain and were now on the down slope. While it didn't get any easier watching Daddy's and Granny's health decline, we at least had Mama on an even keel. We even broached the subject with her that the grim reaper would eventually claim its bounty, Granny and Daddy and when

The Care Giver's Son

this happened, we expected her to move in with us.

The long range plans were to relocate to the beach, build a house with quarters suitable for sustaining two families under one roof. Mama would have her own bedroom and den. We'd share expenses. The plan seemed fool proof.

We were wishing no ill will on Daddy or Granny. We certainly wanted them to be with us as long as possible. Looking at their health issues, common sense just said they'd pass long ahead of all of us, but what do we know about God's real plan.

T. Allen Winn

God's Plan

Christmas just around the corner, Mama had a premonition. Our typical Christmas routine would be to spend Christmas Eve afternoon with my folks, then we'd do the four and half hour drive to the beach to spend Christmas Eve night and day with the grandkids.

Mama asked if we and the grandkids and their parents would spend the Christmas holiday with them this year. She said she wasn't sure why she needed this but felt strongly about our compliance to her request. She told us that maybe it meant it could be either Granny's or Daddy's last one. How could we not agree to her wishes?

Done deal, no argument; we'd be spending the holidays with them then we'd head for the beach Christmas Day after Santa arrived. Three bedrooms in a ranch style house, seven adults and two children; this would be a challenge, but this is what she wanted, so we'd make it work.

Look at me! I had arrived. I had graduated from the University Of WE. Just maybe this was sinking in, or possibly it was just wearing me down. I wasn't ready to pat myself on the back quite yet.

Christmas came off without a hitch. Everyone enjoyed the holiday at Mama's and I made sure we got Granny and Daddy photos just in case Mama's premonitions held true. Everyone survived Christmas.

The Care Giver's Son

After the Santa dust cleared, we consumed our Christmas Day dinner, and then we headed to the beach leaving a happy Mama and Granny behind. We weren't sure how Daddy felt about the event.

We had just settled in at our beach condo, where we planned to spend the next eleven days when we received a phone call the day after Christmas. Our friend, the Home Healthcare nurse, advised us that we might want to come home. Mama had just been admitted to the hospital. Her skin tone had turned yellow and she wasn't able to eat.

We couldn't believe that our beach plans had been interrupted. This was our first chance for such a long stay at our oceanfront condo. Oh well, we packed light and headed back the next day, figuring they'd fix her up and we'd come back and salvage our vacation. We don't always get what we want. It's the life thing again.

We made the typically four and half hour drive back in record time, going directly to the hospital. The hospital was located no more than ten minutes from our house, twenty five from where Daddy and Granny waited for their primary caregiver, his wife and her daughter. Premonitions…

She indeed did look yellow but seemed to be in good spirits. The medical term, Yellow Jaundice would now become part of our vocabulary. We figured it might be something like a gall bladder problem. My wife had gall bladder surgery and had recovered very quickly from it. We remained positive. She had never been prone to illnesses.

A biopsy was scheduled for the next day. We waited for the results. None of us were overly concerned. Mama had always been the perfect picture of health. Her only hospital stay had come years ago when she had a hysterectomy. She didn't go to the doctor for anything.

Out of surgery, the doctor asked to talk to me, her only child. Something didn't feel right about this little side bar he had requested. My wife accompanied me. The cancer word rolled off his tongue. My heart dropped to my feet, my gut did a 360. How could this be so? Okay, my wife was a cancer survivor and medicine and technology had come a long way. How would they treat it?

The doctor told us of all the types of cancers you do not want to have, it just so happened to be that one. It was a type of pancreatic cancer. It had blocked her bowel which explained why she had been having frequent constipation and acid reflux of late. She had complained of back pain but attributed that to her pulling on Daddy all the time.

The caregiver had seen fit to take care of everybody else but had failed to take care of herself. So what could be done we asked? The

The Care Giver's Son

doctor said they had rearranged her innards to be opened up to relieve the blockage and allow her to eat and pass the food through her system. He said an appointment had been scheduled with an Oncologist who could better determine a game plan. She would be fine, right?

With Mama checked into a room, we waited for the plan. My wife and I both stayed at the hospital with her that first night. I remained numb and in shock but knew Mama's track record. This would not sideline her for long. She was too pig headed to let cancer lick her.

During the night as my wife sat there awake with her, this gunk could be seen draining from a tube that had been left feeding from her open incision. My wife, faint of heart, panicked as she witnessed this fluid making its way to a collection canister. She yelled and awoke me from my dosing.

Mama, now sitting up and on the edge of the bed, was nauseated. My wife was on the verge of passing out, something she is very prone to do. Hearing their panic, I now became nurse and rescuer for both of them. Trying to keep Mama from puking all over herself and my wife from falling to the floor, I had my hands full.

I finally eased my wife into the chair I had once occupied, and then I returned with a wet cloth to assist a very sick Mama. Where were all the hospital folks when you needed them? Sure they were good at waking you every hour to check your temperature, but now when we needed them the most, they had vanished.

I finally got Mama stabilized, and then I returned to check on my unconscious wife. I managed to press the alert button and a nurse made an appearance. She took over and restored order. I had already finished the hard part.

The next morning the Oncologist arrived. He tossed us no bone. There'd be no more surgeries. He never mentioned chemo or radiation so where did that leave Mama, us? Doctors don't like to discuss time frames with loved ones or patients but we asked for him to be straight forward with us.

He did. For similar situations the prognosis was typically three to six months. Just a few days ago we were celebrating Christmas. Now this doctor had the audacity to tell me my Mama was going to die and didn't have much time. How could this be happening? She's a rock, never sick and in perfect health. How could this be? No amount of words could express what I was feeling.

As usual, I had made this all about me, my feelings, my inability to deal with it, life being unfair to me. I wasn't dying, I just felt like I was. What about Mama? What must she be feeling? Her concern as always turned to Granny and Daddy. The caregiver had shown through one more time. Okay, time to regroup and deny, deny, deny. Nope, I couldn't pull off

The Care Giver's Son

this deny crap. Mama was seriously ill, but she'd lick this thing because this wasn't how it was supposed to work out. We had our plan.

Mama remained in the hospital for about a week. We almost lost her once to a suspected blood clot. My wife, staying with her, witnessed her sit up in the middle of the bed unable to breath and clutching her chest. Somehow it passed, but after than she had to wear those little leggings and elevate her feet to prevent more potential blood clots. I was learning way too much about the medical profession and illnesses.

We got her settled back in at home and began a new phase in the journey. The once elite caregiver now joined the ranks of the care receivers. Now there were three under one roof. Who do you suppose would be the rising star, the new caregiver? This certainly wasn't something that I was prepared to undertake. After all, I was just a bench warmer. Life certainly can dish out unexpected twist, His plan, not mine.

T. Allen Winn

Raising the Window Just a Tad and Peeping Inside

Neither I nor my wife had fully processed this new information or formulated an action plan. Daddy required 24/7 care. Granny's required care, while not 24/7 yet, tending to her needs had become more demanding. The primary caregiver, now stricken with terminal cancer, would no longer be able to provide this care. We still had Mama's protégée in the picture to help. My wife worked full time and I traveled out of town three days a week. How would we possibly pull this off?

How could Mama have suddenly been stricken with the worse kind of cancer? After further review, we realized it hadn't been quite so suddenly. Warning signs had been swirling, if only we had known how to recognize them. Mama in her pursuit of caregiver perfection had just ignored them. We all wore blinders; me especially. Her back aches, constant bouts with heartburn and constipation had been sounding the alarm bells; and then there was that premonition. Do the math.

And who pulled us from the pits of hell? Who do you think? Mama, she oozed positive thinking. The big C would not lick her. She had way too much caregiving left in that body of hers. Daddy and Granny needed her. It would be as simple as mind over matter. If the doctors

The Care Giver's Son

wouldn't or couldn't treat her, she'd do it herself. If anyone could, she could. She believed. We believed in her.

I began researching the Net to better understand this new disease thrown at my family. I didn't like what I found. Indeed this would not be the cancer you'd wish on anyone. The doctors had not exaggerated the seriousness of it. My hope for her survival diminished considerably, but I didn't for a minute underestimate her tenacity.

Over the next month my wife and I juggled our life, trying to accommodate everyone but ourselves. I continued working out of town. She was trying to commute back and forth from our house and theirs, while keeping her job going. It began to take its toll. We finally concluded that we could not maintain two households and remain sane. Something had to give. Out lives no longer belonged to us.

We decided we had to sell our house. We put it on the market with no expectations of selling it quickly. In less than a week, it sold. On the surface this seemed to be wonderful, but have you ever tried to move your accumulated belongings into one household, where now five adults would be living?

Let's introduce the next diseases to potentially inflict its curse on our little family; mental anguish, mental instability with a dash of stress and depression. Our life, as we knew it, came to a screeching halt, just like Mama's had before us. This would not come easy for us. Following in her footsteps, we did what we felt we had to do. It was the right thing to do, we kept telling ourselves. I'm not sure we fully convinced ourselves. We weren't cut out to be full-fledged caregivers. Who really is?

We experienced plenty of up and down moments. We reminisced. We laughed. We cried. We road that roller coaster for all that it was worth. We battled Mama and her protégée, for control and ownership of the household. Five adults, three generations, all under one roof is a hard row to hoe. To be fair, we set up a co-op, where all household expenses came out of a kitty split five ways (Daddy, Mamma, Granny, my wife and me).

Mama conceded to certain household changes. We replaced our designated bedroom with our own furniture. We converted the living room into our own den/office area. We bought a huge portable storage building, placing it on her property to store most of our furniture and belongings. We utilized a single car detached garage to store everything else. We lived from a single closet in our bedroom.

We did it because it was the right thing to do, but we were not happy campers by any stretch of the imagination. We had given up a spacious new open floor plan home to be cramped in a ranch style twenty something year old house. We made this choice and would live with the consequences for better or worse.

The Care Giver's Son

We eventually overcame most of our frustrations and accepted our inherited responsibilities. It had to be done and doing it rested on our shoulders. We loved Granny, Daddy and Mama, so the decision had honestly been a no brainer. My wife and I had both agreed to this open ended situation.

We had moved my wife's piano into our den, the former living room. Mama loved listening to her play. She played a little too. This turned out to be great therapy for Mama and Granny. They'd cry up a storm when those church hymns were banged out on the keyboard.

Mama died three months after being diagnosed. Like her father before her, she died at home. Granny had outlived her only daughter. Daddy, bedridden, had lost his spouse of over fifty years. I had lost my Mama; something that I had not worked into the equation, or in my head.

Two hours away and in Commerce, Georgia, I had received the phone call about midnight from my wife. I better consider heading home in the morning, she had said. Mama had taken a turn for the worse. Instead, I made the drive in one and half hours after I hung up the phone.

She died sitting on the side of her single bed at five thirty that same morning taking her last breath as I held her in my arms. The last thing she had told me, "I love you sweetie." We suspected a blood clot had been the cause, sparing her a painful and demeaning death by cancer. She was gone just the same. I was devastated.

I had not been there for her when Papa died, but I feel somewhat vindicated. I had stuck in there for her. I thought losing Papa had been tough, but this ranked as the single hardest thing I had ever done in my life. I had never watched anyone die before and now, as an only child, I had watched Mama leave me behind in one single gasp.

Daddy, sharing the same room, had watched her intently from his hospital bed all night. He had not been that alert in years. We'll never know for sure, but in my heart I can't help but believe he knew what was taking place. He never spoke a word or shed a tear, but I know he knew.

We respected Mama's wishes for her funeral, keeping it low key, no big church production, opting to allow our friends at the funeral home to handle everything. Mama so enjoyed the piano and her favorite song was *Amazing Grace*. I had one of those revelations, but I had to run it past some others first. I asked the oldest grandson's mother, if she thought he would play *Amazing Grace* at her funeral. She said for me to ask him. I did. He said, yes. He had never played the organ at the funeral home, so we took him there and completed a test run. At her funeral, a very gifted eleven year old

The Care Giver's Son

played a tribute to Mama, not a dry eye in the place. I'll never forget that moment.

One week after Mama passed, Daddy lost his third brother. We never mentioned this to him. My uncle, born with Down Syndrome, far surpassed his life expectancy. He died in an assisted living facility. Mama had visited him regularly until she had gotten too sick to make the twenty minute ride.

A few weeks before she died, she asked me to accompany her into her living room, our den. There she made me promise that if anything happened to her, I would never place Granny or Daddy in a nursing home and would keep them at home. She hated nursing homes. She had chosen to commit her life to taking care of them at home. She did not allow me to make my own choice. This had been so unfair of her to ask. What else could I do but promise?

Mama, the self appointed one, was now gone. My wife and I were catapulted into the full time world of caregiving, whether we liked it or not. We solicited more help from the protégé. We still had home health care assistance, but without Mama, it had lost its magic. We did what had to be done, but we just weren't cut from the same stone as Mama. Hers were tough shoes to fill.

I had taken numerous photos of that last Christmas and had just gotten them developed. Not until we were looking through them did I realize how few I had actually taken of Mama.

T. Allen Winn

I had focused the photography on Daddy, Granny and the grandsons, not suspecting her premonition would be about her. Ironically, Mama appeared in several candid pictures sitting in the background on the fireplace hearth. Those were my last pictures of her. If only I had known. God works things out while we're taking things for granted.

You can learn new things at any time in your life if you're willing to be a beginner.

If you actually learn to like being a beginner, the whole world opens up to you."
Barbara Sher

The Care Giver's Son

Now Inside the Window Looking Out

Daddy's health neither improved nor worsened, but Granny began to show signs of deterioration. I attribute much of this to the loss of her only child. You're not supposed to outlive your children. My wife shared this same emotional trauma, losing her twenty one year old son to cancer. Things work out for a reason, so they say. I'm not too rational right now. This wasn't the way I had envisioned it. Being an only child with no children, I found it difficult to relate on that level.

All I knew for sure was that this caregiving stuff was much tougher than I had ever imagined. Mama had done it for Papa, Daddy and Granny because she wanted to do it. I let her and now because of the promise, I would do what I was supposed to do.

I had no choice in the matter. She had made sure of that by the promise. Don't get me wrong. I was not resentful about taking care of Granny and Daddy. I was resentful that she put me in this position. My wife, too, felt that she had been very unfair with this request.

Circumstances were much different for us. We both had jobs and up until now, a life. Mama, retired, had chosen her path. We never had that option. I sound disgruntled I suppose, but I would do anything for Daddy and Granny.

I would not go against Mama's wishes. The toughest days of my life lay ahead. Promises…

I think Mama may have possessed her protégé because she seemed to be under the impression that she now ran the household we lived in. My wife and I were accustomed to calling the shots under our roof. After having sold our house, this was our new home, and this was now under our roof. Don't get me wrong, we appreciated everything she did for Granny and Daddy, but we didn't require the same care for our own lives. Too often our wishes fell on deaf ears. I missed Mama and our previous lives.

There was a period when Mama and I were somewhat distant, but in recent years we had grown close; much closer than we had ever been. I could talk to her about everything and often I did. I missed that. I missed her and continued to struggle with her no longer being there for me; to just have had a little more time.

I had given up Daddy long ago. I loved him, but this body he was trapped in no longer felt like my Daddy. Granny, now in her early nineties and with all her health issues, had lived much longer than any of us would ever have anticipated. Mama on the other hand was not supposed to die; not yet. The demons pounded my sorry soul with vengeance. I let them or let's just say I couldn't stop them.

We had experienced many near misses with Daddy over those six years before Mama died.

The Care Giver's Son

He'd always managed to spring back after each brief stay in the hospital, good as ever; ever being as good as he could be in his condition.

Ironically Granny never required an ambulance ride after Mama died. Seems she willed herself to physically overcome her illnesses. I think she believed we had enough on our platter to deal with.

My work continued to require me to be out of town three days during the work week. My wife had to pick up the slack. This strained our relationship and took its emotional toll on her, but we continued to operate under Mama's plan, no nursing homes.

Daddy died three months after Mama. While feeding him his Sunday afternoon diner, his breathing became erratic. Our friend, his home healthcare nurse, just so happened to be out of town when this occurred. Later she'd admit that this had been a blessing for her. It spared her watching him die.

We called frantically for the back up nurse, ambulance, anybody; all in vain. Before my eyes, I had watched my second parent die. I had not signed up for this. I had been sort of forced. Mama had called it a promise. In just ninety short days I had lost both of them. The nurse told us Daddy had aspirated. We had been warned many times that he could possibly go like this. It didn't make it any easier, but I found it easier to let him go than I had Mama.

Daddy had always been a fighter and refused to give in to the grim reaper. This time I didn't see that usual determination in his eyes. He had lost his will to live. With Mama gone, I honestly believe he was ready to join her. In a few short minutes he had.

It hit me like a ton of bricks. I now stood in the same room, lived in the same house where both my parents had died. I had watched both of them take their last breath; something I never wanted to do and had refused to do with Papa.

I didn't know if this was a blessing or my punishment for not being there for Mama when Papa died. I had never been good at this sort of thing, but was learning to be. I did it because it was the right thing to do, not because I had to do it; well, if you didn't count that quilted promise.

I had completed part one of *The Promise*. Daddy died in his own house, only feet from where Mama had. His funeral was kept simple to comply with Mama's wishes.

She didn't like all the fanfare that accompanied the traditional southern funeral and had made us promise to keep hers as well as Daddy's and Granny's funeral very simple. No open coffin, no church funeral, no receiving of friends and family. She disliked making a funeral an event to mark on your social calendar. She had avoided them at all cost.

The Care Giver's Son

Our friend, the Home Health care nurse's husband, had opened his own mortuary long before Mama had died. Mama watched the weekly home town newspaper to keep a tally on the funerals being handled by him and those of his competitor. She really wanted the new funeral home to succeed, often joking how she would contribute to their cause when she, Daddy and Granny passed. We had a good laugh when we told him that Mama had kept up her end of the bargain. Mama would have loved us playing that up.

We weren't out of the caregiving business though. Granny still required our care, but with help from Mama's protégé, we forged ahead. I didn't fully understand it then, but losing both parents in just a short time had been the beginning of dark times ahead for me. Life's lessons still had a few more tricks left in its bag.

Granny began seeing people in her room at night. People she was convinced were real. Now, I'll be the first to admit it. Granny has been the closest person to a Saint I have ever known; a devout Christian with faith running deeply. I thought maybe she was making some sort of connection with the spiritual world. She seemed to have an open line to heaven.

She'd see children with flowers, men and women walking around in her bedroom at night. She'd often call out for us to come in to see them too. Of course we never did witness anyone in the room but her. As a caregiver we are obligated to do these sort of things in the middle of the night; all hours of the night. It goes with the territory, like having small children in the household. Who am I to talk? I have no children. My wife could relate.

On this one occasion while I worked my three days out of town, Granny summoned my wife to her bedroom in the middle of the night. She asked her, "You see them, don't you?" My wife didn't say anything. She didn't want to lie to her and say she didn't see anyone. She wasn't sure how Granny would react if she said she hadn't seen them.

Granny then followed up with, "You have to scrunch down and lean over to one side and then you can see them real good."

My wife somehow managed to diplomatically avoid the line of questioning and convince Granny to go back to sleep. She assumed that would be the end of it. Assumptions, its funny how they never work out the way you assume they will.

The next few days my wife would be tested, but to her credit, she stuck to her guns. Granny recapped the night visit with everyone that graced her presence. She'd end the story each time by saying my wife saw them too, "Didn't you?" She'd just smile and allow Granny to have her say. Oh how we got a lot of mileage and laughter out of that one. You know, you

The Care Giver's Son

really do have to laugh about these episodes or you'd go totally off the deep end.

Mama had died in March, Daddy in July and I now faced my first Christmas without either of them. I still hadn't distanced myself from their deaths. My emotional state suffered more than even I had been willing to admit. Darkness hung over me.

I hated living in their house. They had moved in this home my senior year in high school and I flew the nest after I graduated, so it had never really been my home. Now I felt trapped in their world and they were no longer a part of it.

Traveling down the hallway I had to pass their bedroom. Sure, the hospital bed and single bed were no longer there; replaced by our own bedroom furniture, but still, they had both died in that room. I'm not superstitious or afraid of ghosts. There were just no good memories here. That's just the way I am.

Granny didn't like me traveling out of town and prayed that I would find another job. She does some powerful praying and does have that hot line to the Lord. Searching job openings, I spotted my perfect job on line; the location, the beach, where the grandkids reside. I applied, interviewed and got it. Watch what you pray for Granny. I found a new job.

I'd be starting my job the first week in January. We had my parent's house to sell, had to relocate and purchase a house at the beach.

T. Allen Winn

We also had to break the news to Granny and hoped she'd come with us. She really had no other options.

Problem, she had lived in this one town all of her adult life and now at the golden age of ninety four we'd be asking her to pull up her roots. This caregiver dreaded that conversation.

We decided first things first and delayed the inevitable until we could work out the kinks. We'd place my folk's house on the market first, then find a realtor at the beach and hunt for a home there. We'd break the news to Granny after these tasks were completed. I was in caregiver hell on this one.

As was the case when we decided to sell our own home, we received an offer on my parent's house within a week; even before we officially placed it on the market. We drove to the beach, after lining up weekend sitters for Granny, to locate a new home.

The realtor lined up twenty seven homes for our viewing and we made an offer on the perfect one. They accepted. Now came time to pay the pied piper and break the news to Granny.

I opened with, "Granny, you remember when you told me that you were praying that I found a new job, so that I wouldn't have to go out of town. Well guess what? Your prayers have been answered. Problem is you'll be the one going out of town now." We iced it by giving her an *I Love Myrtle Beach* coffee mug. I asked her what she thought about it.

She answered, "I'm going wherever yawl go." The deal, Granny liking it or not, had been sealed. It went much easier than I had expected. I was one elated caregiver, as was my wife. We asked family and friends to please support this move while in her presence. Most did. With their blessing or not, we were moving.

We decided to have a professional crew move us. We did most of the packing. The challenge would be to time it so that we could take Granny down and make the transition as smoothly as possible. That meant ensuring her bed and her lift-recliner arrived ahead of us. We managed to pull it off.

We settled her into her new surroundings; hers being the second master suite. Quickly we discovered that she teetered on the brink of disorientation. With the new open house plan so different from the confines of the ranch style layout we had just left, she thought the far side of the living room-dinning room area was another house. Like Daddy in the past, we humored her and went along.

Our first priority was to establish a nurse and home healthcare. Then we lucked up and found a lady that could help almost every day with Granny's needs. Everything seemed to be falling in place; much better than we could have ever imagined. We were sort of getting the hang of this caregiver routine after over a year of being in the saddle.

A month into it, things started to go sour. Granny's confusion escalated. She struggled to make the much shorter trip from her bedroom to her lift chair. No longer able to use her walker, we transported her by wheelchair.

She began having bathroom accidents. This had actually started before the move to the beach. Neither my wife nor I were very good at dealing with these episodes. Our new hired hand was excellent, but unfortunately they could not be timed to accommodate her schedule or Granny's.

Granny became very restless at night to the point we installed a baby monitor in her room; the same one we had previously used for Daddy. All hours of the night she'd begin calling for us. I worked full time and my wife still worked from home. We'd swap out checking on her. I was a light sleeper and always heard her first.

Typically there'd be nothing wrong with her. She'd need water which we kept by her bedside on the nightstand or she thought she had to go to bathroom; she still had a catheter. Sometimes she just saw people in the room. Other times she'd be standing by the bed by the time we arrived in her bedroom.

We'd have to talk her back into bed. Soon, after we began to doze once again, she'd begin beating on the wall and calling for help. We'd repeat the routine. The caregivers were at a loss for what to do.

This nightly routine continued for ten nights straight. My wife and I were averaging less than a couple of hours sleep each night during this stretch. Normally I don't take much sleep. I'm typically good on five to six hours each night but my wife takes eight or more. It was taking a toll on us.

I finally realized just how much damage this was doing when by the tenth night I didn't hear her call at all. My wife tended to her and I never knew a thing about it. That next morning I peeped in on her before I left for work at six thirty and she appeared to be asleep.

By the time I had made my twenty five minute commute to work my wife called. She had found Granny sitting in the floor beside her bed in her on excrement; excrement everywhere. My wife could not believe I had left her like that. I explained she had been in bed the last time I checked and was quiet as a mouse.

We had reached our last straw. These two caregivers could not function like this. It wasn't fair to Granny or us. The promise loomed over my head. "Promise not to put either of them in a nursing home." I felt like we'd be the ones going to an assisted living facility if this continued. We were totally fatigued and stressed out. The caregivers were down for the count.

T. Allen Winn

We had no choice but to seek professional help and to explore our options. Neither of us could function like this. As fate would have it, the decision was taken out of our hands. Granny drifted into some sort of coma. The nurse advised us to contact hospice. We did.

The next afternoon I received one of those dreaded phone calls from my wife; similar to the one I had received from her about Mama, and from Mama about Papa. Hospice was there and Granny's breathing had become irregular. I was on my way. This time I didn't procrastinate. I drove directly home as quickly as possible.

We took turns holding her hand and basically paying our last respects. I told her how much I loved her, and that Daddy, Mama and Papa were waiting for her. She had completed her job on this earth.

I returned to our office in the front of the house to discuss our options with the hospice representative. Our hired hand, an angel of a woman, our beach caregiver, sat with Granny in her bedroom, talking to her like she was her grandmother. Our wishes, Mama's wish, we would not send her to a nursing home haunted my every thought. I agonized over that promise.

Before we crossed that bridge we were summoned to Granny's bedroom. She had left us. I had come full circle after avoiding Papa's death. I had witnessed my entire bloodline's

The Care Giver's Son

demise in eleven short months. I had kept the promise. It appeared we were no longer caregivers. I'd give anything to have all of them back.

Granny would be transported back to our home town. She, too, would have the same funeral as my folks before her. She'd be buried by our mortician friend. I could see Mama smiling about that as she added to the tally; one more for the home team.

In the night of death, hope sees a star, and listening love can hear the rustle of a wing.
Robert Ingersoll

T. Allen Winn

Closing the Window but Opening My Eyes

My life had been impacted more in those eleven months than in the previous fifty two years. For a brief period I had walked a mile in the caregiver's shoes. I can't say that it is something I would ever wish to repeat but I am glad I did it. Once staring from outside the window, I experienced it from the inside. I had done the right thing, but only because it was the right thing for me to do. I have no regrets.

The next couple of years would be my toughest. I think they were possibly even tougher than being a caregiver. I'm convinced I succumbed to depression even though I never called on professional help to confirm it. My wife explained to me that I never had a chance to complete one grieving process before being cast into the next one. She was probably right.

While I dearly loved my Daddy and Granny, I missed having Mama around the most. I guess because hers happened so suddenly and it wasn't supposed to be her time. It's ironic that the ninety four year old outlived them all. I still can't believe Daddy outlasted Mama.

I sort of blamed the move to the beach in contributing to Granny's death. She only lived six weeks after we uprooted her. My Aunt made me feel better by telling me she hung in there long enough to make sure I had made the

The Care Giver's Son

move safely and was happy with my new transition. Yep, Granny would do something like that.

My healing process would take a long time. Yes, this time it really is all about me. I feel writing this has helped purge my personal demons. I needed closure and hope this brings it about. If not, maybe it will at least start my personal healing process.

I have learned some valuable lessons from this journey. Never ever take life for granted. It is far too short and precious. I tell others to always cherish that grandparent, parent or elderly relative. Encourage them to tell you stories about their past and life with you as a child. You can never recapture this after they are gone. They have things to say. Listen to them. Never shut them out. What they say and have done is important. When they're gone, it's gone.

Support the caregiver! Support the caregiver! Support the caregiver! They give their all and too often neglect their own health, both mentally and physically. Remember Mama. She ignored her own health. Look where that got her. Caring for a loved one, watching them waste away before your eyes is a tough thing to endure. Those who take on these roles are heroes, but remember, they need your care too.

Ensure the caregiver continues to have a life outside of caregiving. Get them out as much as possible. It is not healthy for them or the patient to be with each other 24/7. Don't let them live the life of their patient. I can't stress the importance of this enough. They must maintain a life of their own. I know. I can honestly say I've been there.

Recognize the martyr syndrome. This is their scream for help. Saying poor pitiful me is not healthy. Put yourself in their shoes literally. Don't be a bench warmer like I was in the beginning. Ask to be put in the game. Be the substitute caregiver. It will change your perspective and life. Don't do it because you have to. Do it because you want to. I know that's not so convincing coming from me. Pig headed, I inherited it, but even a pig can overcome wallowing in the mud if it wants to do it.

Whatever you do, take lots of photos and videos of loved ones before they get sick. You'll want to remember them while they're healthy and not in their deteriorating condition. There's nothing more magical than hearing their voice in that video after they're gone. You tend to forget what they sounded like as time passes. This is a celebration of their memory.

My Wife learned several valuable lessons from being a caregiver. She said she never wanted her children to go through what we had endured. A child should never have to change their parent's diapers and see to their daily bodily functions. She said when her daughter or

The Care Giver's Son

grandchildren came to visit her she wanted them to visit her and not have to take care of her. We invested in long term healthcare for both of us.

Secondly, she said if someone would have asked her she would have told them that there is no way she could do some of the things she had ultimately done, taking care of those who could no longer take care of themselves. She did it. Somehow you find a way to do the impossible.

The internet came in extremely handy, researching Alzheimer's, Parkinsonism, dementia, aspiration, pancreatic cancer, congestive heart failure, just to name a few. Heck, I'd never heard of most of these names and terms. Knowing what you're dealing with prepares you for what's ahead. I caution you, the truth doesn't necessarily make it easier. It's still important to know what you're dealing with, trust me.

If you are the caregiver, please do not make a loved one promise to fill your shoes or do what my Mama made me do. Simple, don't do it! If that person loves you or loves the patient, they will do what is right because they want to do it. A promise made from guilt is not fair for the one that requires the care or the one expected to give it. That decision should come from the heart and that's the way it should always be, unconditional.

I can not thank enough those friends and family members that contributed to my folks' care. They did it because they loved them, not because they had to. They stood by Mama and us through some very tough times. And that's the way it is supposed to be.

Taking the caregiver assistants for granted was probably another one of life's tough lessons for me. I love each and every one of you. You know who you are.

I'd like to think I'm a stronger person for this experience. I would really rather be weaker and have my folks back. It's just not easy watching your entire bloodline be swept away in just a few short months. I am fortunate to have friends and family to help ease the pain. I'm having one of those rambling moments I suppose, so now is a good time for me to wrap this up.

Thank you for hearing me out and being part of my journey. Believe me, I'm not the first and won't be the last to endure something like this. Hopefully you'll be spared.

Don't peer through that window. There's a whole lot of love inside if you hunker down and go inside. Do it because you want to do it. That's what Mama always did. She did it with perfection. I know that now.

It takes less time to do a thing right, than it does to explain why you did it wrong.
Henry Wadsworth Longfellow

The Care Giver's Son

Eating Crow is truly an Acquired Taste

Oh Lord it's hard to be humble, when you're perfect in every way, so sings Mac Davis. No, I'm not perfect, but I have been humbled. Sometimes when you close that window, a door swings wide open in its place. Just when you think you've completed that final chapter, another story needs to be told. Papa died in 1990, easy enough to figure his age as he was born in 1900. My parents passed in April and July of 2004. Granny completed her journey in March 2005. Today, February 10th, 2013, we paid tribute to my Daddy's oldest sibling, his sister passing at the age of eighty eight. My life took another unexpected turn, one I surely never saw coming. Life can offer up surprises, tough love, hard lessons and often a slice of humble pie.

We have established how I am not fond of the hoopla that goes along with a funeral; specifically the wake or gathering of family and friends to pay that last tribute. I have described it as a social event, too much laughter and visiting, with the departed lying within view of the supposedly mourners. I did, after all, inherit that trait from my Mama. Today is that day, the receiving of friends and family at the church for my dearly departed aunt. We will make that trip to Adams Run this morning, a curve in the

T. Allen Winn

road, south of Charleston, between Hollywood and Edisto Beach.

We opted to go to my aunt's home first, where immediate family, my five cousins were gathering. We indeed arrived there shortly after the noon hour, with the receiving of the friends and viewing of the body scheduled between 3:30 and 5:30. Viewing of the body, there's something just too primal in that concept. Walking into my aunt's home was like venturing into a time capsule, nothing had changed since the last time I breached her doorway, probably over twenty five years ago. There were plenty of hugs, tears and yes, laughter.

I had the pleasure of meeting my aunt's caregiver, a black woman who reminded me of a black woman, My Black Mama, who raised me much of my life while my parents worked the second shift in the textile mill. One of my aunt's grandson's had also moved in, co-caregiver he was, and he did it because he wanted to do it. I guess you wonder where I'm going with this.

Today was one of the more memorable days of my life; dread being washed from my thoughts. Today I actually enjoyed being around my cousins, my family and their families in a time of hardship, but yet a time to remember the one we had just lost. This was a unique and humbling experience, coming from one who had thrown stones at what I perceived

The Care Giver's Son

as being the mourning circus, the social event of the day for many. Mark this date on your calendar. I learned today there is nothing wrong with visiting and reminiscing with friends and family, even if it has nothing to do with the loved one or friend lying in that coffin. It is indeed a celebration of life. We did share and swap stories about my aunt, but it went much further, much deeper, and there is nothing wrong with a little laughter at the darkest hour.

I grew today as a person. Just like becoming a caregiver, I took that first step, no longer viewing this as a social event, but instead as something socially acceptable. Life after death can be a blessed event. At almost sixty years of age, I finally get it. Before we departed from the gathering, one of my cousins said to me that he appreciated me for coming. I told him to please not appreciate me for doing this. I could think of no other place I would rather be today. I had done this because I wanted to and not because I had to. Caring is indeed giving. Ironically, as I concluded my above thoughts, a friend emailed me a series of poetic truths, entitled *I Believe*. Several of these hit home I must admit, thus I share them with you.

T. Allen Winn

I Believe....
That we are responsible for what
We do, no matter how we feel.

I Believe....
That our background and circumstances
May have influenced who we are, but,
We are responsible for who we become.

I Believe....
That it's taken me a long time
To become the person I want to be.

I Believe.....
That it isn't always enough,
To be forgiven by others.
Sometimes, you have to learn
To forgive yourself.

I Believe...
That the people you care about
Most in life are taken from you too soon.

I Believe....
That you can keep going long after you think
you can't.

The Care Giver's Son

Putting it into Words, Therapy for the Soul

Everything has a purpose, a rhyme to that reason, or a method to the madness. Sometimes it is as simple as opening that child proof cap and taking a big old gulp of the bad tasting medicine inside. Writing for me is the cure for what ails me. I didn't get here by mistake. Friendly persuasive powers nudged me down the path of no return. How else can one explain that out of the blue, or so I thought at the time, I began writing in that hotel room in Commerce, Georgia. My family was falling apart and I turned to writing as an escape from reality. Six hundred and fifty pages later I had penned my first novel. This was the grooming grounds for what was to come.

When I lost my parents and grandmother in the span of those eleven short months, what did I do? I turned to my writing to fend off depression and mend a hurting heart. Failing miserably as a son and caregiver, writing lead to personal redemption. It was the perfect escape. The plot further thickened in 2010, after we relocated to Pawley's Island. I had occasionally spotted an elderly gent walking his dog in our new neighborhood. We would exchange waves or cordial nods. June of 2011, just after I arrived home from work, the door bell rang, signaling a visit that would pave the road to where I am now, and forever alter my future.

My wife called to me, saying that a gentleman was at the door to see me. It was the dog walker. He introduced himself as Bob O'Brien, a neighbor up the street. He held a book in his hand and had this puzzled expression on his face. He commented, 'You're not Mr. O'Neil, are you?' I replied, telling him we had purchased the home from the O'Neil's. He immediately apologized for his intrusion, adding he had only meant to drop by and show O'Neil that he had published his first book, *The Toppled Pawn*. I told him, 'Interesting, I dabble in writing a tad myself.' He asked if I had a manuscript. 'I have ten completed novels.' He smiled and said, 'Then you and I need to talk. I just started a publishing company, *Prose Press*. We need to get you published.' I looked at my wife and said, 'Is this a sign or what?' Five months later, in October, I held my first published book in my hands, Road Rage, my detective thriller depicted along the grand strand. The following April we published Dark Thirty, my book on bullying.

My point, my parents' sickness probably resulted in kick starting my writing. I scribbled out ten novels from 2004 to 2011, along with about one hundred short stories. I did these for me, not sharing any of them with anyone else. I

The Care Giver's Son

wrote because I enjoyed writing. A move to Pawley's Island, and a gentleman looking for a previous neighbor, leads a publisher to my doorstep and eventually brought to the light of day, *The Care Giver's Son, Outside the Window Looking In*. Tell me there aren't greater powers working here. Without this series of dominos falling, this would have most likely never seen the light of day. I had previously submitted the manuscript to a publisher that features warm hearted, feel good, true stories, but had been told it didn't quite fit them. Touché, I say. I did this for me, not for those who doubted or thought mine didn't fit their mold. It's not always about money.

A person who publishes a book appears willfully in public eye with his pants down. **Edna St. Vincent Millay**

I'm closing by including a short story bonus, *Skinning the Rabbit*. Thank you for lending your shoulders and providing therapeutic heeling for one stubborn and pig headed. Enjoy…

T. Allen Winn

Skinning the Rabbit

TJ skirted the edge of the mangled overgrown hedgerow, its loblolly pines long ago harvested, stumps bulldozed to form a natural refuge for Peter Cotton Tail, slated for tonight's menu. Occasionally snagging his worn Camel brand denim faded overalls on the sharp briers, he trudged along in search of the rabbit boxes he had set just days before.

He loved his Camels, paper thin in places, probably too snug for his two hundred fifty pound frame but still better than those fancy jeans that cost an arm and leg. Other than on Sundays, he wore these overalls like a uniform.

He paused, removed his worn white painter's hat and wiped the beads of sweat from his weathered bald head. Still spry for an eighty five year old, lately he felt the tugs from Mother Nature, reminding him that she still ruled the roost.

Born Thomas Jefferson Davis in the year 1900, third in a family of twelve, he had out lived and buried each and every one of his siblings, the last, an older brother Floyd just three years back. Heart attack got him.

He spotted the first rabbit box butted against a small oak tree. Exhaling, his breath resembled steam from an old locomotive on this cold February morning in upstate Carolina. The Kudzu vine had overtaken the hardwood sapling, claiming it as its own. Locals swore

The Care Giver's Son

you could almost watch it grow and move before your eyes. It provided the perfect home for old Br'er Rabbit.

The box's door had been tripped shut. He could almost taste rabbit for supper but too often he had found the boxes sprung by the wind or maybe a bird. He peeped through the hole exposed by the now dangling wooden trigger.

"Yep, I see you varmint. Caught ya, didn't I? Ya can't hide from old TJ. I can see your gray fur poking outta that hole." He smiled a toothless grin and couldn't help but think of his old buddy Jim. "If Jim was here, he'd give you a what-fer yell. I do miss old Jim. I can't believe that cancer ate him plum up last year."

TJ had buried his wife of 62 years, Ruby Lee, six months before Jim lost his battle. She had been sick, bed ridden for a long time, often not recognizing him. She had died in her sleep. The doctor said her body had just given out, heart just stopped ticking. He called it congestive heart failure.

He and Ruby Lee had made a promise to one another. Neither would put the other in a nursing home. He had kept that promise. She died peacefully in her own bed, TJ holding her as she took her last breath. He loved and missed than woman. It seemed like everybody he loved had just up and died leaving him here alone.

T. Allen Winn

He and Ruby Lee had buried their only child some thirty years back, victim to a drunk driver in a 57 Chevy, running a stop sign. He often thought "it just wasn't right to bury your young'un." Never married, childless, her life had been snuffed out in the blink of an eye. Next week would be her birthday. There would be no celebration.

TJ squatted, tilted the box back, eased open the door and looked inside. "Dag nabbit, sorry ass old black-jack possum, I might have known." Ugly and hissing, the scrawny critter with black tipped hair grabbed a foot-hold inside the wooden box. They were nasty looking but pretty harmless and the butt of southern jokes. The roadways indicated one could never make it across a highway.

"It never fails. I catch one of you varmints every year. Now stop that grinning and hissing at me." These critters weren't known for their manners or good looks.

"Old Jim would pen you up for about a month, fatten you up on milk and bread, clean out that nasty system of yorn and serve you up with taters and onions; that he would. But I ain't Jim."

"I ought to just shoot you and be done with it." He rubbed his hand along the stock of his LC Smith, double-barrel shotgun then shook the box to get old ugly fur-face riled, tilting it until it cautiously peeped out. Lowering the

The Care Giver's Son

gun he watched it exit and slink toward the hardwoods like a gigantic slow moving rat.

"Reckon it's your lucky day, boy. Shells are way too expensive to waste one on you. Now I got to burn this box out to get rid of your stinky smell. Old cottontail ain't going in there no matter how many apples I put in it."

Now, a quarter pass noon, the sun's rays felt good on his back as he checked the remaining four boxes. He had managed to catch a cane-cutter in the last box. Now cane-cutters were ugly critters too, not the pick of a rabbit litter. They lived on the swamp edges, lanky and not too meaty but supper just the same, if you seasoned and stewed it just right. It was old hat with TJ.

Hoofing it back to his army green 61 Apache 10 Chevy pick-up, he loaded the possum's box and cane-cutter in back, and then headed home. Home, a pine frame four room mill hill house sure seemed so huge and empty without Ruby Lee. Driving down South Main lined with ancient red oaks, he somehow missed his turn onto Maple Street.

"Dog gone it, how'd I do that? Guess I'll circle round and come up the back alley." He had made this turn thousands of times and had never overshot it before. Shrugging it off, he hung the next right, made his way up the back alley, common on the mill hill; these single lane dirt roads split the backyards of the houses that backed up to one another.

T. Allen Winn

He skinned his supper with the skill of a surgeon having his method down pat. Snagging the critter's hind legs on two nails on the fence post, he made a couple of well-placed incisions with his pocket knife and skinned him clean in one pull. Gutting his catch, he washed it then cut it up to make it easy for stewing.

Slicing up some taters, carrots and onions, he added about a quart of water, then salt and peppered the chunks before tossing them in the cast iron pot already heating on the back stove eye. Settling down in front of his nineteen-inch black and white RCA, he left supper to simmer. He would have rabbit stew in no time at all.

He tuned in to his favorite shoot'um up, *Gun Smoke*.

"All right Matt, you better watch out cause that gunslinger has got a shotgun over yonder behind them stairs." He often assisted Marshall Matt Dillon in apprehending the outlaw wranglers talking to the TV, enthralled by the on screen antics.

Ruby Lee had always hated westerns, almost as much as she disliked baseball. When not watching a good Cowboy and Indian picture, TJ tuned in an Atlanta Braves game on that super station channel. He liked that young out fielder, Dale Murphy. Shoot'um-ups and ballgames, it didn't get any better than that unless he was wetting a hook at his favorite fishing hole or doing him some serious squirrel hunting.

The Care Giver's Son

Watching the western, he had lost track of time. He sniffed. Something didn't smell good. He sniffed again and tried to focus on that smell spanking his nostrils. He spotted the smoke drifting from the kitchen. Too little water in the pot had charred the stew to the cast iron bottom, ruining his potential supper plans.

He slid out of his lazy-boy recliner with no real sense of urgency and strolled to the kitchen. He stood over the stove for a few seconds, staring at the swirling smoke before thinking he probably needed to remove the pot from the stove. Instead he doused it with his bottle of RC cola making one heck of a mess and almost starting a flash fire.

TJ mumbled, "Something must be wrong with that stove." Luckily he did remember to switch off the stove eye. He and Ruby Lee had always shared the cooking duties, but Ruby Lee wasn't here. TJ was nearly as good at it as her and had always managed to put something together at meal time. Nearly took precedence this time.

"Well, reckon I best open me up a can of Vienna sausage. I reckon there ain't going to be no rabbit tonight." He grabbed a pack of saltines then arranged his meal on the rickety aluminum TV table and quickly consumed supper. The kitchen fiasco had been long forgotten.

Restless, TJ got up and turned the TV channel knob but no program seemed to hold his interest. The plastic molded fake Big Ben clock on the mantel chimed 9 PM. He switched off the television and decided to head to bed, discarding his TV tray and leaving the kitchen in a mess.

His dreams drifted from Ruby Lee to the blackjack possum to old Jim. Big Ben ticked and chimed loudly, warning that father time marched to a new agenda and it didn't weigh heavily in the aging man's favor.

Now early spring, several months had passed since that night the stove ruined his rabbit stew. The old clock on the mantel no longer ticked; the battery now dead and TJ unable to ascertain how to replace it. The calendar now gauged his life spiraling toward an uncertain end. The hour and second hands shed very little meaning to his life.

His boxes had trapped few rabbits. Poor old TJ had been oblivious to the fact that he had failed to bait or check them routinely. Without fresh apple slices inside, un-baited boxes prompted little interest from the rabbit population or a wondering black jack possum searching for an easy meal. Sadly, these events neither concerned nor disturbed him. Most things ceased to matter.

Lonely afternoons were now seldom filled with his favorite pastime, fishing. Either he didn't remember the location of his regular fishing holes or he had just forgotten his love for fishing. He dwelled on neither.

The Care Giver's Son

He had always amazed old Jim with his uncanny ability to sense when the bream were on their beds, pick that particular brush pile where the crappie were hiding, or select the perfect red worms to entice the largest catfish. Now, "amazing" could be simply remembering to go fishing or remembering to do anything that added value to his existence.

When the fish were biting, life had been good. Life wasn't so good right now and it had nothing to with the fish not biting because they probably were if he just remembered to wet his hook.

Something wasn't right. He couldn't quite put his finger on it. It didn't really worry him like it should have. He just muddled through the day the best he could. His best was no longer what it had been.

Alone, he often mumbled his thoughts out loud. "I sure do miss having Ruby Lee or old Jim here to talk to. They'd know what to do. Reckon I ought to go pick up some groceries now? I think it is supposed to be grocery day." He stared at the calendar hanging on the side of the refrigerator. The pages hadn't been flipped in over two months but he didn't seem to notice.

Firing up that old 61, he snailed his way up North Main toward the local Winn Dixie. Traffic behind honked their horns to no avail. He didn't pay the noise any attention. He eventually arrived at the grocery store.

Pushing a wobbly grocery cart matching his wobbly legs, he picked up a half gallon of buttermilk, a six pack of RC Cola, a box of Moon Pies, a couple of cans of Pork and Beans, a loaf of white bread, potted meat, and ice-cream sandwiches. Not exactly a healthy diet but then again healthy eating never seemed to be a priority.

He gave the clerk a wad of bills and walked away not waiting for his change. The clerk flagged him down before he reached the door and asked for two more dollars. He obliged and thanked the kind woman. She smiled and called him Mister Davis. He couldn't remember her name.

He pushed the grocery cart out into the vast terrain known as a parking lot. "Now where's that Chevy?" Rubbing his chin, he finally spotted it three parking lanes over, the driver's side door standing wide open. As he pushed the cart closer he could hear the six cylinders sputtering.

Furious, he started cursing like a sailor. Normally he never used such salty language but normal now eluded him. He had never been a sailor.

"What sorry-ass been messing with my damn pick-up?" Peering inside, he spotted his keys dangling from the ignition. "Hell, they done left my damn keys. I must have scared their sorry asses off."

The Care Giver's Son

Loading the two paper bags into the back, he discarded the buggy in an empty parking space next to a blue Oldsmobile, something he would normally have never done, and then he headed home, sort of.

At home, he reached in the back of the pickup to retrieve the two grocery bags. One bag felt soggy. "Damn, my ice cream done melted!" He tugged the chain of his pocket watch until it plopped from his overalls' pocket. Staring at its face, he shook it then listened for some ticking. The ten minute drive had taken him almost an hour.

"I need to drop this sorry excuse for a watch off to Frank's Jeweler and let Frank check it out. He can fix any thing." Sadly, Frank couldn't fix what was really broken.

He carried his groceries in the house on shaky legs, put them away, placing the melted ice-cream in the freezer compartment of his Frigidaire. Troubled, he flopped down in his worn and tattered lazy-boy and stared at the television's empty screen. He didn't bother to switch it on but didn't recall why.

"What's the matter with me? It just don't make no sense, no sense at all. Ruby Lee will make things right when she gets home from the mill," he kept telling himself.

A light frost glistening on the lawn now marked fall's approach and TJ's eighty sixth birthday. Both passed uneventfully. Life in just seven or so months had become a vicious daily struggle. It scared the crap out of him, most of the time. He simply existed, trapped in a too often mindless body.

He had recently managed to flush his store bought teeth down the toilet and laughed as he watched them swirl and disappear. "I don't need them teeth anyway," he remarked to justify his actions, "I got gums of steel. Shoot, I can eat anything anybody else eats. My choppers just get in my way. All I got to do is mix and mash it up on my plate. It's all going down to the same place, ain't it?"

Newspapers and magazines were stacked two feet high atop the stove. Luckily, he no longer cooked. When he ate, he ate directly from the containers. Those discarded cans and boxes cluttered the kitchen table and counters. The trash had not been taken out in over a week. He paid little attention to the stench.

Dirty clothes were piled in the bath tub. Baths were no longer part of his routine. He wore the same filthy Camels, forgetting to wash them too. His body odor simply mingled with the odor swirling from the accumulated and aging garbage.

The phone had long been disconnected, just a nuisance anyway. He had little contact with people except when he ventured to the grocery, now only about once every couple of weeks, when he remembered to go. The strangeness smothered him like a wet tarp but, unable to

The Care Giver's Son

react or comprehend, he withdrew until it passed.

Church folk still dropped by, bringing him hot meals, calling them meals on wheels. He thought what a funny name. He always met them at the door and would not let them enter his house. He didn't know why he did this because he had always welcomed company in the past, but he didn't dwell on it.

His meager monthly social security check supplemented his not so demanding life style. He sometimes even remembered to pay his bills. What didn't get paid got either cut off or discontinued. He never read the final notices. Most of the time he forgot to get the mail from the box.

A self employed painter most of his life, he had failed to report most of his earnings and paid very little taxes. Ruby Lee had tried to encourage him to pay taxes but he didn't trust Uncle Sam. Most people paid him in cash so Sam didn't get his cut. He and Ruby Lee had always managed to pay their bills, a little down, and a little along, they managed just fine.

The State Farm agent had often tried to persuade them to buy something called long-term health care insurance. He had told them the insurance would make sure that they were taken care of if something bad happened to either's health.

Pig headed, TJ had always said "*Insurance, just another waste of our money. We got each other and Ruby Lee's mill insurance. Long as we can breathe, ain't nobody putting us in one of them nursing homes to rot! We promised we wouldn't let that happen."* He had kept his promise to her, but who would keep her promise to him? He seldom dwelled on it now.

The nights or time just before dusk tormented TJ. A fear brewed as twilight approached. He didn't understand the dread but it had a name, Sundowner's Syndrome. He paced the floor until perspiration dripped off his beaked nose, clothes becoming soaked. He fretted over it.

"I got to get out of here before the people come home and catch me here in their house." The dreaded sundowners caused him to sincerely believe he occupied a stranger's house and they would return home and catch him there like a common criminal. He had no one to tell him right from wrong, real from imaginary. If he thought it, he believed it.

These peculiar thoughts too often filled his head. What was happening? Why was it happening? Why was it happening to him? Then he'd forget what he had just thought.

Rabbit season had once again arrived. With it came time to set out the boxes. This had always been something TJ looked forward to but this year he just couldn't seem to embrace it. The task had become lost somewhere in that brain of his.

The Care Giver's Son

One afternoon he stared at the boxes stacked in the old shed, but they meant nothing to him. He finally shrugged, walked back in the house, opened an RC and munched on a Moon Pie. He gazed at the blank TV screen seeing only his reflection. The television, on or off, didn't seem to make much difference. Little meant much to him most days.

Two weeks into rabbit season and no rabbit boxes had been set. He had his good days and bad days. The bad days were winning hands down and so were the rabbits with no traps set to catch them.

A month into rabbit season and just after the first real hard frost, TJ sat on a tool chest in the shed staring at the stack of wooden rabbit boxes one more time. "I know I'm supposed to make this right. This here cold spell means I'm supposed to...I know I am...supposed to." He nodded his head to confirm it but confirm what?

He eased up from his sitting place and shuffled out into the yard. Funny, he seemed to be shuffling a lot more lately, steps not true and sure, and strides too short. Getting from one place to the other took much more time with those baby steps, but what was time now? He had long ago misplaced his pocket watch.

He rubbed his hand along the hood of the 61 leaving a smudged streak, his old pickup filthy and neglected. He wiped his hand on his overhauls, also filthy and neglected.

T. Allen Winn

He spoke out loud. "Truck, you and me got to go somewhere, don't we? Yeah we do." He stood there trying to will himself to think, but with his head empty of any significant thoughts, he just walked away, again. The world was a much safer place without him on the roadways.

He did his little shuffle walk over to the skinning post. He touched the nails and some sort of fuzz clung to his fingers. He picked at it and examined it, and then wiped it on his overhauls. It became just another of the unidentifiable stains and substances on the denim.

The post, crimson with dried critter blood, didn't register as anything that should mean something. He knew it should but it didn't. Many a critter had been skinned by him here, but that was then and this was now. Unfortunately neither now or then registered in his memory.

An odor filled his nostrils, a foul smell. He sniffed and fanned the air, oblivious that it came from him, too long without bathing and wearing those stinking overalls. Making his way back to the house he clutched the back stair rails with both hands, laboring to make the six step climb. His motor skills were non-existent most days.

Even though the stove clock displayed half past noon, all the lights were on throughout the house, TV blaring in the background as Ernie

The Care Giver's Son

Johnson and Milo Hamilton hosted the pre-game show for the Braves-Dodgers baseball game on that super station.

TJ eased into his recliner, sipped on a warm RC and ate a half eaten, stale Moon Pie while the game played on. Dale Murphy slammed a homer but it meant nothing. The Braves won the game handily. TJ was now in extra innings and losing.

Rabbit season half over; the boxes collecting dust and still stacked in the dilapidated wooden shed, symbolized his world now hopefully lost. The rabbit population thrived. TJ had no recollection of rabbits.

Out for a stroll, Preacher Reese spotted TJ in the back yard sitting in his hand crafted cedar swing, suspended from the hundred year old red oak. TJ actually managed a grin recognizing the long time preacher. He had attended very little church since Ruby Lee's death. He had gone because it meant something to her.

"Well, howdy Preacher." He yelled out to the approaching portly man

"Thomas Davis, how have you been doing? I don't believe I've seen you in the Lord's house in quite a while, now have I?" The stench from TJ's soiled overalls and soured body overwhelmed his senses, but Preacher's expression never changed.

"Doing okay I reckon, Preacher. No, I don't think I been to church since Ruby Lee..."

Unable to finish the sentence, he just stared at the Preacher, unaware that he had stopped in mid sentence.

"Suppose you won't be inviting me over for that famous fried rabbit of yours," insinuated the Preacher

"Rabbit... Preacher?"

"The boxes, I noticed them over there in the shed. You didn't put them out this year? Didn't Ben Buzhart let you use that back forty of his again?"

"What... Preacher?" Asked TJ, trying to focus on the questions

"Yes sir, I do believe this is the first time I remember you not setting them out on his farm. I always look forward to those fixings of yours."

"Rabbit boxes, the rabbit boxes, I need to put out them rabbit boxes, them in the shed," mumbled TJ.

"Probably not too late, weather's just about right. Do you need any help with them?"

"Nah, I think I can do it, Preacher. I really appreciate what you done."

"Thanks, for what? I don't recall doing anything, my friend?"

"The rabbit boxes, reminding me about them rabbit boxes."

"Son, we all forget. Our minds aren't as young as they used to be. What do they call it? Oh yeah, having a senior moment. I do have quite a few of those moments myself."

The Care Giver's Son

"You don't understand Preacher. I didn't forget to set out them boxes. I just plain didn't remember what they were. I knew I should, but I didn't."

Preacher Reese felt like he had been hit between his eyes with a sledge hammer, seeing first hand what life had dished out to his friend. He placed his hand on TJ's shoulder, said a sweet prayer and told him he'd be checking on him regularly.

"I'll make sure the congregation brings you those hot meals and helps you with your laundry. You'll be in our prayers, Thomas. I'll drop back by tomorrow."

"Meals on wheels," grinned TJ, bidding the Preacher farewell.

He nodded as he picked up a rabbit box and studied it, rubbing his hands along the edges of the rough wooden frame. "God bless my soul, I know what they is!"

Now late afternoon, he loaded each of the rabbit boxes into the bed of the 61. Shuffle gone, he entered the house, grabbed his fateful double barrel and truck keys. He remembered what to do. He had a little pep in his steps.

Propping the shotgun by his side, he pulled the truck's choke and throttle, eased his left foot onto the clutch and patted the gas as he turned the ignition. The old truck grunted, coughed, and sputtered black oil-laden smoke but did manage to crank. He eased it into reverse and backed out the drive, didn't hit anything for a change. He remembered how to back up and how to drive. "Ye-haaaaaaa!" he cried out

Thankfully he recalled the route to Ben's place, drove down the back road along his property line as he had done so many times before. He parked the 61 at the edge of the field and surveyed the hedgerow where he'd be placing the boxes. He smiled, proud that he had even remembered to stop by Finley's produce stand to pick up some apples for baiting the boxes. He felt rejuvenated and alive.

One by one he set out the boxes until only two remained. It felt like old times. He returned to the 61 to retrieve those last two and grabbed that old LC Smith double-barrel. He set the first box, rubbing the apples around the box's entrance, then threw a couple of cut pieces inside and set the trigger to the door. Pausing, he wiped the sweat from his head with a nasty handkerchief from his Camel's back pocket.

Walking to the swamp's edge with the last box, his stride had become noticeably shuffled. He entangled his feet in the Kudzu vines and almost fell. He squatted by the box and stared at the funny looking black strands of fur inside; remnants of old black-jack's last short stay. He had not remembered to burn out the box.

"Come on, let's don't forget now!" snorted TJ. Things were jumbled in his brain, making no sense. He shook his head trying to shake the cob webs, but still he couldn't recall, had forgotten his purpose for being here. He stared at the shotgun resting against a stump then peered back at the rabbit box. Blinking he recalled something and smiled.

"LC, old buddy, looks like it's me and you now. You remember the promise, don't you? We promised no nursing home!" He rubbed his hand along the two shinny black barrels, smiling and humming Amazing Grace. Finally his thumb came to rest on the shotgun's safety. He clicked it off and thought salvation. "Promises, Ruby Lee, we vowed to keep our promises. I kept mine."

Preacher Reese had stopped by the next morning as promised to check on his old friend, Thomas Davis. After knocking, he had found the house empty with Thomas and his truck missing.

His neighbor last remembered seeing him load the rabbit boxes in his pickup and drive off late yesterday afternoon. He hadn't noticed that the truck had not returned until the Preacher had mentioned it.

Playing a hunch, Preacher drove to Ben's farm. After explaining the situation to Ben, they headed to the hedgerow. They followed the trail of rabbit boxes, soon locating Thomas Jefferson Davis sitting on a stump, his back to the hedgerow, with his shotgun across his lap, fingers still resting on the duel triggers, eyes wide open and glazed over.

Ben reached over and felt for a pulse. "I think he's dead, sir. The safety is off on his shotgun. It looks like he wanted to fire a warning shot. I wonder why he didn't."

Preacher Reese smiled, "Ben, God bless his soul, the Lord always works things out. I believe our dear friend remembered the right thing to do just in the nick of time, and then that old body of his just finally gave out, just like his wife's before him. He's with his Mrs. Ruby Lee now."

"Look over yonder, sir, that rabbit box is tripped shut. Looks like ole TJ might have caught himself one last rabbit. Fitting don't you think? We could have one last stew on his behalf."

Preacher diverted his eyes towards the heavens, smiled and nodded in agreement. "One last supper," chuckled Preacher, "Now doesn't that seem profound?"

Ben slid the rabbit box's door open and they both peeked inside. Grinning and hissing, an ugly black-jack possum grabbed a foot hold inside the box. It seemed to focus on TJ perched on the stump behind them. It, too, remembered.

Ben tilted the box, tapped on the side and the possum reluctantly exited. "Get," said Ben, "Before I'm tempted to empty his shotgun on your ugly ass."

"Two of God's creatures have been saved today Ben," exclaimed Preacher Reese,

The Care Giver's Son

"Mysterious ways, they never cease to amaze me."

"Whatever you say Preacher," replied Ben. "You call the ambulance and I'll collect the remaining rabbit boxes."

Looking to the heavens, Preacher Reese took a deep breath then closed the old man's eyes one last time.

"Lord, only you could have known there's more than one way to skin a rabbit."

How to build a rabbit-box-trap:

http://www.ehow.com/how_4487921_build-rabbit-box-trap.html

T. Allen Winn

PROSE PRESS

The origin of the word prose is Latin, *prosa oratio,* meaning straightforward discourse.

Prose Press is looking for stories with strong plots. We offer an affordable, quality publishing option with guaranteed worldwide distribution.

Queries: E-mail only.
proseNcons@live.com

www.ingramcontent.com/pod-product-compliance
Lightning Source LLC
Chambersburg PA
CBHW031246290426
44109CB00012B/457